EGYPTIAN
ONE-ACT PLAYS

Selected and translated from the Arabic by

Denys Johnson-Davies

HEINEMANN
LONDON

THREE CONTINENTS PRESS
WASHINGTON D.C.

Heinemann Educational Books Ltd
22 Bedford Square, London WC1B 3HH
PMB 5205, Ibadan · PO Box 45314, Nairobi

EDINBURGH   MELBOURNE   AUCKLAND
HONG KONG   SINGAPORE   KUALA LUMPUR
NEW DELHI   KINGSTON   PORT OF SPAIN

ISBN 0 435 90232 6 (AWS)
     0 435 99418 2 (AA)

Published in the United States of America 1981
by Three Continents Press
1346 Connecticut Avenue, N.W.
Suite 1131
Washington, D.C. 20036

ISBN 0-89410-237-0 (paper)
     0-89410-236-2 (cased)
LCN 81-51660

*The translator acknowledges with thanks
financial help from UAR National Commission
for UNESCO*

Set in 9 on 11 point Times
Printed in Great Britain by Fletcher & Son Ltd, Norwich

Contents

Introduction

The question 'Did the Arabs have a theatre?' has provided the subject for
a number of books, doctoral theses and learned articles, from which it is
clear that there are any number of answers to the question, depending on
the conclusion one wishes to reach. The one short answer to the question
– if by Arabs we mean the Arabs before they became acquainted with
Western culture, and if by theatre we mean what the Western world
understands as theatre – is: no. For reasons largely religious and
sociological, the Arabs developed no form of fiction, and prejudice
against it still exists today among the religious. The domain of the
theatre and of fiction is, in general, man's struggle to make sense of his
own existence, of his fellow men and of his environment, to describe and
analyse the various situations in which he may find himself, to seek
solutions to the moral questions with which he may be faced and, not
least in practice, to deal with that growing industry of the West, romantic
love. Thus for the pious Muslim invented tales are inevitably at best a
waste of time, fit reading matter only for women and children, and at
worst irreligious artefacts that can only stir up doubts about issues that
have already been clearly established. It is not surprising, therefore, that
the Arabs of old, who were so active in translating the works of Greek
science and philosophy, should have found the comedy and drama of the
ancient Greeks unworthy of their attention.

It was, of course, from Europe that the dramatic form was first
introduced into Egypt and other Arab countries. In Egypt this came
about as a direct result of the country's exposure to Western influences
through Napoleon's short sojourn there and through Mohamed Ali's
practice, later adopted by his successors, of sending educational missions
to Europe. The stages by which the dramatic form entered modern
Arabic literature were, logically, first translation, then adaptation and
finally original composition. Thus in 1848 Molière's *L'Avare* was
performed in translation, and in 1873 an Egyptianised adaptation of
Tartuffe under the title *Sheikh Matluf* was produced by Uthman Jalal. In
rendering the play into Arabic, the translator exercised his own
considerable linguistic and inventive talents, a practice followed, some

seventy years later, by Nagîb al-Rihani, a comic actor of genius who, together with his collaborator, produced a number of free adaptations of little-known French farces, clothing them in the social and political circumstances of Egypt under the late king and the pashas, with Britain as the 'unwanted guest'. The plays were adapted with skill and humour, exploiting the rich colloquial language of Egypt. This tradition is still very much alive today and may be seen in the political satires of Yusuf Idris or in the work of Ali Salem, who is represented in this volume.

A difficulty peculiar to a playwright writing in Arabic, as to the Arab writer of novels or short stories, is that of language. As Arabic has two forms – the written, which is common to all Arab countries, and the spoken, which differs from country to country – the writer is faced with the dilemma of choosing which language to write in or opting for a mixture of the two (as many short-story writers and novelists do), selecting the written form for the narrative and the colloquial for dialogue. The problem is more complicated than it may appear to the outsider, however, in that it involves not solely an aesthetic choice but also serious political and religious considerations; the classical Arabic language is a powerfully unifying political force and also the language of the Koran and thus of Islam. Where the theatre is concerned, the general position is that comedies are written in the spoken form of the language, historical plays in the classical form and other kinds of drama in either form, depending on the nature of the play, the characters portrayed and the preference of the writer. An indication of the reluctance of writers to make use of the colloquial form of the language is to be found in the painstaking translations into classical Arabic made by the late Mahmoud Teymour, pioneer of the short story in Egypt, of certain plays that he had written in the colloquial language – thus showing, in the clearest possible way, that classical Arabic is no vehicle for comedies about present-day peasants. Tewfik al-Hakim too has been taken to task by the critic Louis Awad for having failed to use the colloquial language in most of his plays, though it should be appreciated that in his early years he had employed the dramatic form merely as a frame for the philosophical and social themes with which he was concerned and that these plays were not written with performance in mind. It is arguable, however, that more recent plays, such as *The Tree Climber* (regarded by many as his masterpiece) and *Fate of a Cockroach*, both plays in modern settings, would have benefited from being written in the spoken rather than the literary language – though in the case of the latter it might be held that if it is permissible for cockroaches to talk at all, they should do so in the classical language. It is interesting to note that among the playwrights featured in the present volume Alfred Farag, most of whose writings have been in classical Arabic, is enough of an artist to see that *The Trap* would have run the risk of deteriorating into pure melodrama if it had been written in the classical language instead of in the dialect of Upper Egypt, where the play is set. In fact, all the plays in this collection were written in the spoken form of the language, which differs from area to area, from class to class and from period to period – in a language, in short, that is dynamic.

The Egyptian theatre is a serious theatre; the influences on its playwrights are Brecht, Beckett, Ionesco, Weiss and Pinter rather than Noel Coward and Terence Rattigan. Without exception, they all have a keen political and social awareness, and most of them, understandably, are leftist. The domestic farce, the musical, the whodunit and the thriller are as yet unknown, though spasmodic viewing of Egyptian television indicates that such genres are in the process of becoming part of the entertainment offered to viewers.

Translators have shown even less interest in the Arab theatre than they have in Arabic fiction generally. It therefore seems pointless to give a list of names of those playwrights whose works are not available in translation, although mention should perhaps be made of one or two writers who do not feature in this collection. Yusuf Idris, many of whose short stories have been translated, has already been mentioned; he combines a sophisticated technique with an unrivalled handling of the nuances of the spoken word. Another name of importance is that of Nu'man Ashour, a committed naturalistic playwright whose portrayal of characters at all levels of society is wholly convincing and whose aim is avowedly social criticism from a Marxist standpoint. Finally, mention should be made of the poetical drama, pioneered by no less a figure than Ahmed Shawqi, Egypt's 'Prince of Poets'. Its exponents today include Abdul Rahman al-Sharqawi, whose novel *Egyptian Earth* was translated and published in London some years ago, and the poet Salah Abdul Sabbour, a translation of whose play *The Tragedy of al-Hallaj* (the Sufi mystic who was put to death in the tenth century) has been published in Cairo.

Of the plays in this collection, Farid Kamil's *The Interrogation* takes us back to the events of Suez, presenting the Western reader with the opportunity of seeing this incident from an Egyptian viewpoint. Alfred

Farag, the author of *The Trap,* is best-known for his full-length historical plays, which treat of subjects taken from the early history of Islam, the Pharoahs and heroic resistance to the French occupation of Egypt under Napoleon; in the short play by which his work is represented here he deals with a story of crime and treachery in the Egyptian countryside. *Marital Bliss* by Abdel-Moneim Selim is the least 'Egyptian' of the plays and clearly testifies to the influence of such Western writers as Ionesco. In *The Wheat Well* Ali Salem exploits a humour that is universal in his swipes at the bureaucracy that is the most recent of Egypt's deadly plagues. Tewfik al-Hakim's play is an adaptation in dramatic form of one of the well-known stories about the wise fool Goha and is another illustration of his thesis that a folkloric literature of the absurd has long existed in Egypt; it also celebrates that gentlest and most maligned of animals, the donkey, of which this playwright is known to be fond.

The theatre in Egypt – and in other parts of the Arab world – is now firmly established; it is to be hoped that with time more translations of the works of Arab playwrights will become available to the reader of English.

Notes on authors

Farid Kamil was born in 1931. He studied for two years at the Higher Institute of Fine Arts and held several exhibitions before deciding against making a career of painting. Having studied journalism at the American University, he joined the Cairo Office of United Press International and was later the East European correspondent of the Middle East News Agency, living in Belgrade. Besides a series of studies on Egyptian art, he has published numerous short stories and two novellas. *The Investigation* was one of his first attempts at the dramatic form.

Alfred Farag, born in Alexandria, graduated from the English section of Alexandria University. He worked as a teacher, then as a journalist and cinema and theatre critic. His first published play, *The Fall of a Pharoah*, appeared in 1957. From 1963-6 a state grant enabled him to devote all his time to writing and in 1966 he joined the Theatre Organisation at the Ministry of Culture as Literary Adviser. He first made his name with *The Barber of Baghdad*, a comedy inspired by the Thousand and One Nights. Most of his plays – *The Trap* is an exception – are written in the classical language. Many of his plays deal with incidents from Arab or Egyptian history and have been widely performed throughout the Arab world.

Ali Salem was born in 1936 and studied at Ain Shams University and the American University in Cairo. He has been connected with the theatre for his whole working life and worked for a time as an actor. He specialises in writing comedies that have political significance. Perhaps the best known of his full-length plays is *You Who Killed The Beast*, a political variation on the Minotaur theme. A recent play, *B.A. in Ruling Peoples*, a satire on emergent nations and their rulers, was put on in Cairo in 1979. He has adapted a number of plays from the French and also writes film scenarios.

Abdel-Moneim Selim was born in the province of Rosetta in 1929. He studied law at Cairo University and worked as a tax inspector in the provinces and later in Cairo. From 1962–7 he lived in London and travelled widely as the correspondent for one of Cairo's weekly magazines. On returning to Cairo he and a group of his friends set up a theatre called 'The 100 Seat Theatre', showing original and translated work of an experimental nature; the play *Marital Bliss* was first performed there. A short story by him, *The Lost Suitcase*, appeared in the translator's volume *Modern Arabic Short Stories*.

Tewfik al-Hakim was born in Alexandria in 1902 and began writing for the theatre as a student. Sent to Paris to complete his law studies, he became more determined to make a career as a writer. On returning to Egypt he was appointed to the provinces where he gained the material for his novel *The Diary of a Country Magistrate*, published in English translation in 1946 under the title *The Maze of Justice*. He later resigned from government service and devoted himself to writing. He has written nearly a hundred plays, several novels, as well as short stories and volumes of essays and memoirs. He has been a major influence in Egypt and the Arab world generally, especially in the theatre. Most of his major works have been translated into French and other European languages. In English, however, apart from the novel mentioned, which is now out of print, the only works of his available are a volume of two full-length plays and two one-act plays, published in the Arab Authors series under the title *Fate of a Cockroach*, also the play *The Tree Climber*, published in 1966 by Oxford University Press; like the short play by which he is represented here, *The Tree Climber* shows his interest in the Theatre of the Absurd.

Denys Johnson-Davies was born in Canada in 1922 and studied Arabic at London and Cambridge Universities. He worked in the Arabic section of the B.B.C. for several years and more recently was the director of a radio station in the Arabian Gulf. He has published a number of translations from modern Arabic literature, most of them available in the Arab Authors series; he is also co-translator of two volumes of Hadith (the Sayings of the Prophet). He lives in Cairo.

The Interrogation

Farid Kamil

The Interrogation *by Farid Kamil*

Cast

MAN

WOMAN

Set: *The curtain is already raised on a darkened stage. The scene is a room which looks bare because of the paucity of furniture. To the right is a large desk on which stand an old-fashioned telephone, a lamp, a hand megaphone, and an old radio. Behind the desk is a vast, imposing chair; it has a multi-coloured cushion on it which is the sole spot of colour on the stage. Behind the chair is a tall, spindly hat-stand, like a leafless tree, on which hang an army cap and a tarboosh with a shiny brass badge. In front of the desk is a hard, high-backed chair. On the wall facing the audience is a light-coloured rectangular space where a medium-sized picture had been hanging, while to the right and close to the desk is a calendar showing the date, Tuesday, 6th November, without the year being specified. To the left of the stage is a door. This opens in the direction of the auditorium so that the audience are unable to see who opens it or is standing behind it unless someone actually comes on to the stage. On the right wall, that is to say the wall opposite the door, there is a window behind the desk. This is so close to the auditorium and the audience that when the man stands up to talk through the window, it looks as though he is addressing his words to the audience in the auditorium.*

The sound effects are in the main made up of the noise of rifle fire and explosions, and these are heard from time to time throughout the play; the more violent explosions may sometimes be accompanied by lighting effects, such as flashes at the window or the electric light going out and then coming on again.

The time is midnight. The door opens and the man enters, leaving the door open behind him. He presses the light switch: the stage is lit up and at the same instant the auditorium grows dark. The man turns round towards the door.

HE: Come along, woman. Come in. [*After a while, with a derisive bow*]
   Please come in.

The woman enters slowly and fearfully. She looks around her at the room.

SHE: [*Mumbling*] In the name of God the merciful the compassionate.

*The man shuts the door behind her. He goes up to the calendar to change
the date so that it becomes 'Wednesday, 7th November'. He goes towards
the desk looking at his watch. He takes up the megaphone and makes
towards the window till he is standing in front of it facing the audience. He
takes a piece of paper from his pocket and reads it out into the megaphone
in a stentorian voice.*

HE: A notice to the inhabitants of the city. People, on Tuesday morning the
   Military Governor issued a military order to the effect that any person
   found by the security forces to be in possession of arms or explosives will
   be liable to summary execution.

*Directly the man has finished reading the military order a projector, either
from behind the scenery or from the prompt-side, projects on to the wall
facing the audience the name of the play, the author, producer, actors and
so on. At the same time the man re-reads the notice once or twice until the
titles of the play are over.*

HE: A notice to the inhabitants of the city. People, on Tuesday morning the
   Military Governor issued a military order to the effect that any person
   found by the security forces to be in possession of arms or explosives will
   be liable to summary execution.

*The man is about forty years of age; he has a raucous voice and a face full
of lines and wrinkles. He wears native dress which is, however, of excellent
quality: a galabia, a skullcap with a turban wound round it and army
boots. Later in the play he will lift up his galabia and it will be seen that
under it he is wearing the uniform of a British Tommy: wide shorts down to
the knees and puttees up to below the knees. He will also change his
headgear from time to time.*
    *The woman is of about the same age. She is rather thin and is dressed in
the clothes worn by the poorer classes in the industrial towns. Her face*

*combines an expression of tragedy and great gentleness. Her hair will
become gradually greyer as the play progresses until, at the end, it will be
completely white.*

    *The titles come to an end and the man finishes reading the notice into
the megaphone, which he places on the desk. He wipes at his sweat as
though having made a great and exhausting effort.*

    He turns round to the woman.

HE: Please sit down and make yourself comfortable – there's the chair. [*He
    points to the chair facing the desk, then turns round to take off his
    skullcap and turban and hangs them up on the hat-stand. Again he
    turns round to find that the woman is still standing where she was*] Sit
    down, lady.
SHE: No, I'm fine like this, sir. You sit down and make yourself
    comfortable.
HE: No. No. You sit down and make yourself comfortable, woman.
SHE: I'm quite happy like this . . .
HE: [*Interrupting her and shouting*] Sit down.
SHE: [*Startled*] Certainly, sir. [*Looks around her hesistantly*]
HE: Here, on this chair. [*Points to the chair*]
SHE: [*Hesitatingly*] But I'm quite happy as . . .
HE: [*Interrupting her and shouting*] Sit down.
SHE: [*Seating herself in trepidation on the edge of the chair and
    stammering*] Certainly.

*The man rises to his feet in front of her and stares at her for several
seconds. She is too frightened to move. The man, walking round the desk to
his chair, turns and continues to stare at the woman.*

HE: Have we come here to play games, woman? Do you think we've come
    here to play games? There are no games played here. You may be
    playing games at home but not here. Understand?
SHE: I understand, sir.
HE: You're to sit absolutely still without moving. I shall do the talking and
    you're to sit still and not open your mouth unless I tell you to.
    Understand?
SHE: Yes, sir.
HE: Good. [*He seats himself slowly on the chair and tilts it back, while
    looking at the woman searchingly*] First, do you deny the charge?

SHE: As you say, sir.

HE: [*Abruptly seating himself upright in the chair*] What d'you mean by 'As you say'? When I ask you a question you're to answer it . . . and quickly. Are you denying the charge?

SHE: I don't know, sir.

HE: What d'you mean you 'don't know'? How don't you know? After all, didn't they find the bombs in your house? Didn't they find them right there in front of you and take them out in front of you from under the bed? . . . or were you struck blind at the time and couldn't see?

She does not answer.

HE: Did you or did you not see? [*She is silent. He shouts*] Answer.

SHE: [*Lowering her head*] Yes.

HE: Yes what?

SHE: Yes, I saw.

HE: What did you see? Did you or did you not see the bombs when they took them out from under the bed? [*She is silent*] Answer.

SHE: Yes.

HE: Then you admit everything?

SHE: No, sir.

HE: How do you mean 'No'? Didn't you see the bombs when they took them out from under the bed? Then you admit you had the bombs in the house under your bed? Who put them there? [*She is silent*] Where did these bombs come from? Where?

SHE: I don't know, sir. By the Prophet, I don't know.

HE: So you don't know anything about anything? Are you just plain stupid or are you putting on an act for me? Something in your house and under your bed and you don't know where it came from? [*She is silent*] You heard the announcement over the megaphone? You heard the notice that's being broadcast every hour and that I just gave from the window? What does this notice say? Someone in whose house bombs or weapons are found, what do they do to him? Say . . . what do they do to him? [*She is silent*] H'm? Do you know or don't you? Do you know?

SHE: Yes.

HE: What do they do to him? Do they marry him off? Do they give him a pay rise? No? They execute him. That's to say they kill him. One of two things happens: either they hang him [*He acts this by placing his hands round his throat*] or they fire a few shots at him. [*He points his finger at her and shouts*] Bang! Bang! Bang! Yes, they execute him. The military order gets issued yesterday morning and where's the first place they find bombs? Under the good lady's bed. Now, do you understand what this means? Bombs mean execution. Bombs under your bed mean whose execution? Whose do you imagine? [*She is silent and he shouts at her*] Whose? [*She does not reply. The man jumps to his feet, and she does too, while the man shouts at her*] Have we come here to play games? We've said there are no games played here. Here it's bombs and executions, not games. Understand? Sit down.

SHE: Yes, sir. [*She sits down while he remains standing*]

HE: God save us, what sort of animals are these?

The man strides up and down the room, coming to a stop from time to time to stare at her. He goes to the hat-stand and puts the cap on his head, then returns to the desk and seats himself on the edge of it opposite to her. He lifts up his galabia in order to show part of his British uniform.

HE: Listen here, woman. Those English aren't joking, they mean business. 'Yes' means 'yes' . . . [*The slide projector shows the translation*] . . . and 'no' means 'no' [*The projector shows the translation*] Yes, they're straightforward people and can't be fooled . . . not by you or a hundred like you, nor by the red djinn themselves. Why? I'll tell you why. Firstly, they're a civilised people . . . people with a civilisation and traditions and morals, with lords and a beautiful queen and the lot. How can we compete with them? They didn't build up an empire from nothing. This empire of theirs is magnificent, it takes in the world from one end to the other. The sun never sets on it. Where do you think they got all that from? D'you think they inherited it from their fathers or won it in a lottery? No, they got it by know-how and brains, by diplomacy and force and being civilised, also by being tough and hard-headed.When an Englishman wants to do something he does it. If he wants to fly in the air he sits down calmly and drinks tea and smokes one of those cigarettes of his and then makes himself the finest of aeroplanes and off he flies in it. Those people are something altogether different . . . a race quite apart from ours. And along you come, you animal of a woman . . . excuse me for saying it, you who call the water-buffalo 'mother', and want to make fools of them. Many a cleverer person before you has tried it. They stayed in our country seventy or eighty years and we didn't know how to get them out. What

did Saad Zaghloul say? He said 'It's no good'. We turned
them out and back they came. It's no good. Do you want to turn them
out, you and those idiotic children of yours who call themselves
fedayeen? How are you going to fight them? With the bombs under the
bed? Are you going to fight them from bed, woman? [*He tickles her and
laughs*] Ha! Ha! If you were a bit prettier and had a little more sparkle to
you we'd have said you'd take the whole British army into your arms
under the bed cover and you'd explode the bombs and blow them all up
and be done with them. Ha! Ha! You mad woman . . . who could do
such a thing? Who talked you into this nonsense? Who fooled you and
brought you the bombs? Where did you get them from? Did the fedayeen
give them to you?

SHE: I don't know, sir.

HE: You don't know. Fine. We'll see now whether you know or not.

*He gets up from in front of her and walks round the desk. As he passes the
hat-stand he hangs up the army cap and takes the skullcap and puts it on.
Then he seats himself in his chair and takes out a pen and some paper
from the drawer of his desk and prepares to write.*

HE: Is there anything you want to say before I open an official enquiry?

She is silent.

HE: Have you a card or proof of identity?

SHE: Yes. [*She hands him a card*]

HE: [*Talking as he takes down the details from the card*] Name . . . Age . . .
[*Raises his eyes to her*] Thirty-six years old, woman? Now why don't
you give up that sort of humbug? [*He goes back to taking down the
details*] Date of birth . . . Place of birth . . . [*Raises his eyes*] If you were
born in Tora what ill wind drove you along here? Why didn't you stay
on there making life a misery for them instead of honouring us with your
presence here? Address . . . [*After taking down the information
contained on the card he scrutinises the photograph*] This your picture?
You look really very pretty. You must have bribed the photographer.
Ha! Ha! Ha!

*He gives her back the card, then continues with the interrogation, writing
down the questions and answers.*

HE: Do you admit that the bombs were found at the flat you occupy at the above address?

She does not answer.

HE: Why don't you answer? . . . surely we've finished with this point?

She does not answer.

HE: God Almighty, I swear by Almighty God three times, woman, that if you don't answer I'll write down what replies I like and get you into real trouble. Are you going to answer or not?

SHE: As you say, sir.

HE: You admit they found the bombs in your flat? [*She hesitates and he shouts at her*] Answer.

SHE: Yes.

HE: [*Writing*] Do these bombs belong to you?

SHE: No.

HE: Then whose are they? Is there anyone else living with you at home?

SHE: Just myself and my children.

HE: How many are there?

SHE: Two.

HE: Their names and ages.

SHE: Khairy's at the university . . . may your children also go there . . . and Shuhdy's at secondary school.

HE: Their ages?

SHE: Eighteen and sixteen.

HE: And their father?

SHE: He cleared off.

HE: Where's he cleared off to? Is he dead?

SHE: I don't know. He cleared off long ago.

HE: Cleared off. By the Prophet, I don't blame him for clearing off . . . you're enough to scare away a whole town. Anyone else living with you at home?

SHE: No.

HE: Is there anyone who comes to the house regularly?

SHE: No, sir.

HE: What d'you mean by 'No, sir'? You've admitted they found the bombs under the bed and you've admitted there's no one else who goes into the bedroom except you and your two boys, then it only stands to reason that the person who put the bombs there was either you or one of the boys, isn't that so?

SHE: No, sir.

HE: [*Extremely angry*] Still 'no'? All right then . . . let's see where this story of yours takes us. [*Continues the interrogation*] How long have you been living in this flat?

SHE: For three years.

HE: Was your husband with you when you rented it or had he already cleared off and got rid of you?

SHE: He wasn't with me.

HE: Did you rent it furnished?

SHE: No, sir.

HE: Absolutely empty?

SHE: Yes, sir.

HE: Sure? That's to say, when you rented it there was absolutely nothing in it . . . not even just a few bombs placed on the floor in the bedroom waiting for your bed to come along and be placed over them?

She does not reply.

HE: Why don't you answer? Were there bombs in the flat when you rented it?

SHE: I don't know, sir.

HE: Of course you don't know . . . how should you know? You rented the flat empty. You got the flat, took over the keys and along came the furniture on a cart. You put it into the house, placing the bed in the bedroom which no one enters but yourself and your boys. So the person who brought the bombs was either you or Khairy or the other one, whatever his name is.

SHE: Shuhdy . . . may the Prophet protect him.

HE: Or Shuhdy . . . isn't that right? Answer . . . or are you once again going to say 'I don't know'?

SHE: As you wish, sir.

HE: That's new! Bravo! Well done! [*He strikes the desk with his fist*] You've driven me mad, woman . . . may God bring down your house on top of the bombs in it. Just explain to me: What do you want me to do about you? Shall I strangle you with my own hands and take the consequences, or shall I lift up the receiver and tell the Major you've confessed and let them kill you and spare me the trouble of you? Eh?

She does not reply.

HE: Animals! God knows where they get you from. Coming from Tora are you? By the Prophet, wouldn't it have been better if they'd put you in Tora Penitentiary instead of letting you plague us down here? Now what made you leave Tora and come to us here? Tell me your story from the beginning . . . or don't you know that either?

SHE: Not at all . . . there's no story or anything.

HE: Speak, woman.

SHE: Certainly, sir. I'm speaking aren't I? I . . . I was brought up by my uncle, the fact being that my mother and father were killed in an accident when I was small.

HE: Of course . . . people like you bring disaster to their parents.

The woman recounts her story as though in a dream. The light on stage can be slightly dimmed. The woman both stands and moves as though asleep, unaware of the interjectory sentences which the man sometimes utters. While she is telling us the story of her marriage the projector shows on the back wall five different pictures of her working-class husband, who resembles to a certain extent the man interrogating her. In the first picture he appears as a laughing young man; in the second as putting on a serious air; in the third as conceited, cold and cruel; in the fourth he has let himself go, his chin is unshaven, his clothes unkempt; in the final picture he has a blank, hopeless expression. When the pictures have been shown the light returns to normal on stage.

SHE: [*Continuing*] He brought me up with his children. When I was seventeen years old he married me off to his eldest son. [*The first picture is shown*] He had just begun to work in the company at a good daily rate of fifteen piastres. I had the same affection for him as for my own brother and after less than a year I had Khairy.

HE: So you didn't have quite the same affection for him as for your brother.

SHE: [*Unaware of the interruption*] After two more years I had Shuhdy. We were living well, thanks be to God. They were happy days and we lacked for nothing in the world. We were sheltered by God's goodness and we had the children . . . what more could one want of Him? But the man . . . the children's father . . . got greedy. When he was young he used to tell on us when we were naughty, and when he grew up he began telling on his fellow workers and would report things about them to the Pasha who was the director: so-and-so has gone and done such-and-such a thing; so-and-so has been saying such-and-such things; so-and-so is inciting them to strike. The trouble they had with his tale-telling to the director! The Pasha conferred on him the price of treachery . . . he became a shift leader and everyone knew him for what he was. Whenever he went in anywhere the conversation would come to a dead stop, and whenever anyone said a word to him or smiled at him it was simply from fear of his slanderous talk or in the hope he'd give him a bit of promotion or a pay rise. The locals ignored us: those with whom we'd eaten bread and salt no longer used to say good morning to us. How often I did advise him, 'Father of our children, your fellow workers will be around longer than all the country's Pashas and foreigners,' and he would say to me, 'Woman, I'm doing it for the children. By the Prophet, if it weren't for the children I wouldn't do it. This is good fortune that has come to us and who refuses good fortune when it falls into one's lap?' Finding himself with more money, he started drinking and smoking hashish to excess. My reason said to me, 'Father of my children, I'll be leaving you,' but my heart said, 'How can I leave you? Aren't you my husband? Aren't you my cousin and like a brother to me, also the father of my children? Aren't you everything I've got in this world and aren't you all that's left to me and the children? Maybe too there's even something to what you say.' Days passed and along came the Revolution. The foreign owners of the factories smuggled their money out and escaped. The Pasha who was the director tucked a few thousand away and went off to Lebanon and the children's father found himself on his own. The government came along and appointed a new director. The children's father sucked up to him and passed him information. Who was he fooling though? His comrades had pinned him down for what he was and the new director, aware of his past, knew him for an opportunist, for someone who served anyone above him, anyone with power or money in his hand. The fact is that's a type that's well known and always gets found out and however long he lasts he always come to a bad end eventually. However much he screams and shouts he's still known for what he is . . . even those he sucked up to turned against him. He found himself as lonely as a stray dog in the

town. The whole town knew about him and they'd turn their faces away
when he passed so as not to have to exchange greetings with him. A stray
dog in the midst of the town. He left his work when he became so
disliked that people began insulting him. He found nobody to go to,
nobody to say a kind word to him. Also he was no longer able to find the
money to buy hashish. Then one day he went out in the morning and
didn't return. He disappeared. [*The final picture in the series of pictures
of the man disappears*] They said he'd gone off to Cairo to look for work
in some place where no one knew him. I said to myself 'I'll go on waiting
for him. I'll wait for him.'

HE: [*Fascinated by her story*] And then?

SHE: The children were older . . . Khairy was fifteen and Shuhdy
seventeen . . . and many was the time they'd return from school crying
and saying 'We've been insulted by our schoolmates.' You see, children
hear things from their parents and repeat what they hear to other people
without thinking. Some days the children would be crying and I'd say to
them 'Patience is the best cure . . . tomorrow the town will forget.' Then
I'd go out and find them quarrelling with the other children. One day
Shuhdy came to me with his face covered in blood and his clothes torn.
He said one of the children had said to him: 'You son of a coward, you
son of a spy, you mother's boy.' He called him every name under the sun
and he kept silent. Then the children said: 'Of course you're a coward,
the son of a coward . . . where's the man you could take after?' One word
led to another and then they set about him and beat him up. I said to
myself 'There's no life for us in the town,' so we left Tora and came here.
[*She turns towards the man*] I work in people's houses; in the mornings
the children are at school and in the afternoons they learn a trade at a
garage and earn a few coppers: Khairy's become a mechanic and
Shuhdy's a welder and body sprayer. When they grow up, God
willing, they'll open a garage and repair shop on their own. O Lord,
grant them long and successful lives . . . for the sake of the Prophet, O
Lord.

HE: [*He stands up and walks towards her as she stands in the middle of the
stage*] Gracious! Gracious! You really have had a very tough time. You
deserve better luck. [*He makes clicking sounds with his tongue*]
Gracious! Somebody like you . . . only thirty-five years old, in the very
bloom of youth . . . a mature and experienced youth . . . and pretty too!
By God, you really do look exactly like the photo on the card. The
photographer did a good job. [*He laughs*] If only, though, you were to do

your hair nicely . . . [*He fondles her hair*] . . . and were to dye the odd one or two white hairs you have and put a little black on your eyes and a little red on your cheeks and lips, you'd really blossom out . . . by the Prophet, you'd be as good as new. [*He pats her on the cheek*)

SHE: [*Pleased at his compliments*] Ha! Ha! By the Prophet, you shouldn't make fun of me, sir. I've had it, I'm past it. As the proverb says, 'What will the hairdresser do for an ugly face?'

HE: What d'you mean by 'ugly', woman? By the Prophet, you're more beautiful than a full moon . . . you're just like new. You've had two children but your figure's full and as firm as a rosebud. [*He tries to fondle her body*)

SHE: [*Smacking his hand and laughing*] Good God, whatever next! It seems you're a real devil.

HE: [*Clapping his hands*] The Devil looks after his own. Get what I mean? By the Prophet, someone who looks like you, a real good-looker like you, why didn't you remarry when that good-for-nothing husband of yours took off?

SHE: [*Coyly*] I? Get away with you! D'you think I'm one for that stuff? Heavens no!

HE: Is there any woman in the world who's not for that stuff? Good God! We're more than up to it. Come on, wake up. Good God . . . after all we're only flesh and blood.

The telephone on the desk rings. The man jumps up in evident terror. He takes up the receiver and talks into it; the magic lantern shows the translation of his words on the opposite wall.

HE: [*Into the telephone*] Hullo. Yes sir. [*The magic lantern shows the translation*] One o'clock. I am very sorry, my clock's not working. [*The magic lantern shows the translation*] Yes. Yes. Now. Very sorry. Very sorry, Major Sir. All right. Goodbye. [*The magic lantern shows the translation*]

He returns the receiver to its place and hurries to the window as he takes from his pocket the piece of paper so as to read it through the megaphone.

HE: A notice to the inhabitants of the city. People, on Tuesday morning the Military Governor issued a military order to the effect that any person found by the security forces to be in possession of arms or explosives will be liable to summary execution.

He returns to the desk, places the megaphone down and takes out his handkerchief to mop at his sweat as he looks angrily at the woman.

HE: You were going to land us in a real mess, God damn you. All right then, by the Prophet I'll show you what for.

He takes off the skullcap and throws it on to the hat-stand. He seats himself in the chair, puts his feet up on the desk, exposing a part of his uniform, and talks extremely quietly.

HE: The fact of the matter is you don't understand what working with the English is like. No one understands what working with the English is like. Those English are straightforward people and mean what they say . . . once they say a thing they don't repeat it. They're dead serious . . . no nonsense or playing around. If someone serves them they reward him well. They give him money and they invite him to tea and biscuits and they give him leggings like these ones. [*He points to the puttees he is wearing*] Also they take him off to London in the middle of the fog to meet their Queen and they give him a right royal time there. If you serve them well and honestly they build you up and help you and take you with them to England. But in return for this reward they want work: they want you to work with them properly. What I mean is, it's no easy matter. Also, it's not as if just anyone can get along with the English. Not everyone's smart enough to give and take with them and to know how to deal with them. Those English aren't fools, and don't imagine I'm just wallowing in their generosity, or that they're old dodderers and that I'm simply wiping up their dribble for them. God Almighty, I'm really killing myself with work. Every day from early dawn I'm interpreting for the Major and going off on inspection tours and doings swoops with the Sergeant and making announcements in Arabic to the people . . . and, as you can see, here I am at 1.15 in the morning sitting and working my head off with you. The whole day it's like that. 'Zainati, come here.' [*The magic lantern shows the translation*]'Zainati, go there.' [*The translation is shown*] The whole weight of responsibility lies completely on my head.

SHE: [*Moving towards the desk with slow steps*] May God help you and give you strength and grant you success.

HE: The fact is they can't find anyone else they can rely on to help them. There's lots of work and lots of demands on me. One doesn't know how to get through the work here or look after the bellies at home that must be filled every day and which don't understand there's a war on with bombs and things, that houses are being destroyed and people dying. No sooner do the children wake up in the morning and open their eyes than they're opening their mouths too and saying 'Daddy, we want to eat. Daddy, we want to eat.' What shall I give them to eat? Shall I tell them 'Hang on, children, till the war ends'?

SHE: [*Sitting down*] The Lord God Almighty forgets no one.

HE: That's fine talk that is. If I said it to my children, by the Prophet they'd eat me up. The fact is it hurts one to see the poor little things wanting something however small, and in order to get it for them everything else in the world is of no importance. Yours truly was a real good longshoreman. I used to sell to the boats passing through the Canal: the odd camel saddle, the odd pouf, the odd Nefertiti wallet. Now the Canal's blocked and the children have only me. Tell me, by the Prophet, what can I do? They say Zainati's buildings are the most beautiful, all full of marble they are. You see, the two white buildings along the sea belong to me . . . may you have the like. What they're envying me for I don't understand . . . the children came from God and the buildings from the sweat of my brow. We smuggled the children out of the house all right, but how are we going to smuggle out the buildings? Perhaps some stray shell, amidst all this random bombing, will bring them to the ground . . . and then do you want my children to die of hunger? By the Prophet, if it weren't for my children I wouldn't be doing this.

SHE: [*Angrily*] But everyone's children are hungry and no one's prepared to work with the English. All the children are hungry . . . no bakeries working and no restaurants, no grocers' or butchers' shops open. Everyone goes to bed on an empty stomach. You're talking like my children's father. D'you think it's just your children's bellies that are so delicate?

HE: What's wrong, woman? Have you gone crazy or something? By the Prophet, you're absolutely dotty. You won't put only yourself into real trouble but me too. The fact is you don't understand a thing . . you're like a cracked waterskin, the words just ooze out of you.

SHE: No, by the Prophet, I understand everything fine. I understand this story and know it off word by word.

HE: What story?

SHE: You understand and so do I.

HE: By God, you understand absolutely nothing. That chair you're sitting on understands better than you. Is this head of yours stuffed with pebbles?

She looks at him defiantly while remaining silent.

HE: Woman, the military order came out yesterday morning and in the afternoon they found the bombs under the bed at your place. The whole town knows they found the bombs at your place and after two or three hours an execution will be carried out in the city's main square so that everyone will be given a lesson and know that the English are men of their word. Understand? The English are now in a position from which they can't retreat. This means that, God willing, in a manner of speaking they'll be obliged to execute some man or woman in order to justify themselves in front of the people. It's in my interest and in yours that they execute someone worthwhile . . . somebody other than a poor wretch such as yourself who's like a blind cat that can't walk about without tripping over her feet. Woman, why can't you understand? We want to co-operate together so as to get you out of this fix those bastards have got you into. We want to save you and see that justice is done and the real criminal is punished. Where did you get the bombs from? Who brought them and put them under the bed?

She does not answer and continues to stare at him defiantly.

HE: [*Walking quickly to the hat-stand, putting on the tarboosh, then returning to her*] I can of course call a couple of soldiers to take hold of you and beat you up till you confess to everything. We've got all sorts and kinds of torture: we can beat you with a rubber hose, or break your ribs, or hang you up by your fingers, or burn you with hot irons, or put things into your body, or immerse you in water till you're about to drown; we can bury you in the middle of the cemetery till you go mad, put red pepper inside you, or stick pins under your nails. We've got a thousand and one ways, and when they take you off to execution nobody'll think of saying 'See whether she's been tortured or not.' Would you like me to call a couple of soldiers to make you see sense or will you confess nicely and decently without any fuss?

She does not answer.

HE: The English don't care whom they execute or whom they don't. Be careful not to imagine you're of any concern to them. What are you to them? . . . An ant, a fly, a louse. Be careful not to imagine the English came all the way from London just for you. Do you think they care if you're tortured or not? All that matters to them is to find out how the bombs came to be with you so they can get hold of the source . . . it's the source that's important. It's not important if ten or a hundred people are tortured or die just so long as we get to the source. The Major, though, doesn't like torture because it leaves marks. In London they've brought torture down to a fine art: electric shocks, blowing you up with water, drops of water on the head . . . can you imagine, the Major says this method makes the toughest man go mad in less than an hour? But I've got a better method than beating and torture and dripping water . . . a marvellous method no one's thought of till now. [*He approaches her with a smirk*] Would you like to know about it?

She does not answer. The man walks round the desk; he turns on the desk lamp and directs the light so that it falls on her face; he brings it nearer to her. Then he approaches closer to her across the desk till his face is directly in front of hers.

HE: I'm certain it's not you who are responsible for the bombs and so we're not going to execute you. [*He stops walking for a while*] We'll execute one of your children. [*She lowers her head and he seizes her by the chin and raises her face towards his*] Which one of your children would you like us to execute? [*A moment of silence*] Khairy? [*A moment of silence*] Shuhdy? [*A moment of silence*] Which of them do you love the less? Which one are you prepared to sacrifice for the other? The eldest or the youngest? . . . motor mechanic or welder? Eh? [*He is silent for a moment, then lets go of her head so that it falls on to her breast. He leans back in his chair and pushes the tarboosh forward on to his head*] I want you to choose for us the one we're to kill.

A moment of silence, then the woman bursts out crying, her body heaving and shaking. The woman weeps bitterly while the man is leaning back in his chair, his tarboosh pushed forward on his head. He regards her in silence.

HE: What do you think about that? If you're not going to tell us who gave you the bombs, then, my dear, you can choose us one of your children to execute.

SHE: [*Sobbing and wailing and clutching at him*] I beseech you, sir. Do what you like with me. Kill me, but leave my children alone. God keep and prosper you . . . after all, you too have children.

HE: Tell me where you got the bombs from and I'll let you and your children go.

SHE: I don't know. I swear by Almighty God. I don't know. By the Holy Koran, I don't know.

HE: Such talk will do you no good. It's getting on for two o'clock and I want to let the Major know the name of the person responsible for the bombs before I announce the military order. This time it's I who'll be ringing him up. If you don't tell me who gave you the bombs I'll be forced to tell him the name of one of your sons. [*Shouting at her*] I'll make them put one of your sons to death . . . they'll kill one of your sons.

The woman rises to her feet and cries out at the top of her voice. The moment she begins speaking and until she finishes the magic lantern projects on to the wall facing the audience a series of pictures of executions by hanging and firing-squad taken from unusual angles: tilted, concentrating on small details and so on.

The woman can be standing between the magic lantern and the wall so that a portion of the picture shows up on her while the rest is projected on the wall with her shadow in the middle.

SHE: [*Shouting*] Kill me! I'm ready to be put to death. Open up my collar and prepare me for the gallows! [*She opens her collar*] Lay open my breast to the bullets! [*She opens the front of her dress*] I'm not frightened of death. I've already had my days on this earth and am of no more use. But the children . . . have pity on the children. Kill me! Kill me in their stead! Execution? . . . what does execution mean? Isn't it just death? Isn't it better than a lingering illness, than the wheels of a train? For the Prophet's sake, kill me! If there's any pity in your hearts, kill me instead of the children. [*The pictures of execution come to an end*]

HE: Enough! When I say something I mean it. Either you choose one of them or I'll kill them both.

SHE: [*Bitterly*] Why not kill all three of us?

HE: [*Seizing her by the shoulders and shaking her roughly, while he shouts and pushes her before him to the middle of the stage*] Being funny with me are you? D'you think I'm joking? Playing a game are we?

SHE: [*In the centre of the stage*] God will have His revenge on you. God willing, what you do to my children will happen to yours. [*Her arms are raised skywards*]

HE: [*Shouting*] Don't move! Keep your arms up like that! Any movement from your arms will decide which of your children will die. The right arm is Khairy, the left Shuhdy. Any movement of your right arm and Khairy dies, any movement of your left and Shuhdy dies. Let's see which arm moves first.

SHE: [*Her arms are raised and her fists clenched as she speaks through tightly closed teeth*] O Lord God . . .

HE: [*Interrupting*] If you move your head to the right it'll be Khairy, to the left Shuhdy [*Her head is held motionless; he passes around her*] If you move your eyes to the right it's Khairy, to the left it's Shuhdy. If you move any part of your body to the right its Khairy, to the left it's Shuhdy.

The woman is standing motionless in the centre of the stage. Her arms are raised high, her fists clenched, and the light is centred on her. The man walks round her as he talks. Passing the hat-stand, he hangs up the tarboosh. From time to time he walks towards the woman to direct his words at her.

HE: Yes, that's nice. You've become a statue and you've shut up, but do you think you can stay like that for long? How long can you stay without moving? Five minutes? Ten? Only too soon you'll get tired and whether you like it or not you'll find yourself moving, and any movement by you will have its victim: Khairy or Shuhdy. Your muscles have obviously begun to ache. Your arms are as heavy as though filled with lead. Your back's eating into you and you've got pins and needles in your legs. A drop of sweat will run down your face, a fly's just about to settle on your ear. It'll go right inside. You'll move. You'll move. Any movement you make however small means that either Khairy or Shuhdy will be put to death. Or you can confess to everything and save yourself and us any fuss. [*He tries to surprise her*] Look at the door! [*She does not move and he laughs*] Ha! Ha! You're a clever one all right . . . you didn't even move your eyes. [*He walks about for a while then comes to a stop in front of her*] What does one call what you're doing now? Stubbornness? Obstinacy? Stupidity? Or do you think it's patriotism? Let's hope you're not thinking it's patriotism? What's patriotism done for you? Isn't that just what got you the bombs under the bed and brought you here today? What's patriotism to us? We got all het up and threw out the English and now the English have returned and the French have returned and Israel has taken Sinai, the Canal's blocked up, houses have been destroyed, a few thousand have died, and we've ended up in a worse state than before. All that's been done for patriotism. Can we do a damn thing by ourselves? Each one of us is at the other's throat. After all, you know what sort of person an Egyptian is: you scratch my back and I'll scratch yours. He'll bite the hand that feeds him. Do him a favour and he'll ride you . . . and swing his legs around. All he's good at is bribery and corruption and putting on airs. An Eyptian's no damned good for anything at all, and so one's just forced to think of one's self. One's got to be clever and wide awake and watching one's own interests, to be sharp and all there. One mustn't let one's luck slip away . . . one must ride on the wave as it's coming in and always be with those who are on top against those who are underneath; one must make one's voice the very loudest, so loud that it drowns anyone who might show you up. And when the wave begins to sink down you must jump off it on to the one that's coming, and so again be with those who are on top against those underneath. It's I who lay down the rules of the game and you who go along with them; it's I who hold the thread of your life and that of your children and you who don't dare even make the slightest movement lest it mean the death of one of your children. [*While walking round her, he finds himself directly behind her. He stands there and suddenly shouts*] Bang! Bang! [*She does not stir*] You're really clever! Bravo! You've got nerves of steel!

Suddenly the door of the room is opened and a voice from behind it calls out.

VOICE: The wireless! The wireless! [*The door is closed again*]

The man hurries to the wireless set and turns it on. He stands beside it and hears the following broadcast given in an animated voice.

WIRELESS: An urgent report from New York states that Mr Dag Hammarskjöld, Secretary-General of the United Nations, has today held an extraordinary press conference at which he suddenly read, breathlessly, the note of the British and French delegations accepting the ceasefire in Egypt as from eight o'clock this morning. The governments of Egypt and Israel have accepted unconditionally the ceasefire in accordance with the resolutions of the United Nations. Informed diplomats have commented on this report by saying that the acceptance by Britain and France of the ceasefire is an admission by them of the failure of their venture to invade Suez. These diplomats predict that the British and French forces will be withdrawn from Egypt in the near future and that the Israeli forces will be withdrawn from Sinai directly an international emergency force has been formed. Mr Hammarskjöld read out at the press conference the text of the note of the British and French delegations, which is as follows: 'If it is possible for the Secretary-General to confirm that the Egyptian and Israeli governments have accepted unconditionally the ceasefire and that the international force which will be formed is capable of guaranteeing the aims contained in the resolution of the General Assembly of the 2nd November last and to supervise them . . .'.

The telephone rings. The man turns off the wireless and quickly answers the telephone. He talks in English and the magic lantern shows the translation of his words on the back wall.

HE: Yes, sir. [*The magic lantern shows the translation*] Yes, I heard it on the radio. [*The magic lantern shows the translation*] Is that true? [*The magic lantern shows the translation*] Withdraw from Port Said and go back to London? [*Translation*] I am very sorry you go back to London. [*Translation*] I am always at your service. Please remember that very well and tell everybody in London. [*Translation*] Tell everybody Zainati is at the service of Great Britain. [*Translation*] At your service any time you come back. [*Translation*] Yes, goodbye. Thank you. Goodbye. [*Translation*]

He puts back the receiver and stands as rigid and motionless as the woman. From afar is heard the noise of an approaching demonstration chanting patriotic slogans.

HE: [*Talking to himself as though in a dream*] The English are going. Now the people are looking for me, they'll single me out; now the people will kill me. [*He walks up and down the stage in a state of great agitation, then comes to a stop*] It was all done for my children. [*He puts on an act of weeping, perhaps moistening his finger with his tongue and tracing two tears below his eyes as he talks in a choked voice*] It's for my children . . . if it weren't for my children I'd never have done anything. My children wake up in the morning and open their eyes and mouths and say, 'We want to eat, Daddy.' [*He takes a couple of steps, then comes to a stop*] I'll say to them [*He takes up a heroic stance and talks in a loud, stentorian voice*] . . . I'll say to them: 'I . . . [*He strikes his chest with his fist*] . . . it's I who saved the country. I worked with the English so as to save innocent blood, so as to end violence and killing and destruction while preparing for the English to be turned out again by peaceful and legitimate means. I . . . [*He strikes his chest*] . . . I'm a hero and it's due to me you were able to do something no one else could. I worked with the English and softened their hearts and it's due to me that you're all alive today to rejoice and celebrate. [*He takes a couple of steps, then comes to a stop*] I'll say to them, [*Pompously*] 'I had some long sessions with the English and after discussions and negotiations I was successful in persuading them that they were wrong. If you'd just given me a bit more time I'd have got the British army mutinying against their Queen.' [*He takes a couple of steps, then comes to a stop*] I'll say to them [*Quietly and fawningly*]: 'They said they'd take me to London in the middle of the fog, that I'd meet their Queen and that she'd give me a garter like this one [*He raises his galabia to show his leggings*] and they were going to make me "Sir" . . . Sir Zainati. They fooled me, they tricked me, they pulled the wool over my eyes, they took me for a ride, they turned my head, they played on my feelings and exploited my kindheartedness and innocence, the sons of dogs . . . they did all this to me when they found I was just a longshoreman who understood nothing about politics or war. I understand nothing about anything. They saw I was an ass and they fooled me. It was my fault . . . you're quite right to blame me. Let me kiss you all on the head and let bygones be bygones. [*He blows two kisses into the air*] Bless the Prophet, [*Proudly*] we're all Arabs after all and generosity's in our nature and nobleness and gallantry are attributes for which we're famed. Also we've got this thing about foreigners . . . we always do what we can for foreigners and give in to them; if one of them takes advantage of us we say "Never mind" and if he slaps us in the face we say "God will take revenge on him. Your day will come, you oppressor." We say "The Lord does not forget his worshippers. Every man shall be done by in accordance with his deeds,

and if the English think themselves powerful it's clear that God
Almighty is more powerful than them. He'll make things hot for them
and give us revenge against them." As for us, we're the most generous of
people, we do what we can for the stranger and give in to him.' [*He takes
a couple of steps, then comes to a stop*] I'll say to them, 'Those people
threatened me . . . one of them was a great large fellow with twirled
moustaches and he was holding in his pocket a revolver as big as
anything and he stuck it in my back. I either had to obey them or they'd
have let me have it, I'll say to them: [*He looks around cautiously as
though about to disclose some important secret*] 'I was given the task of
spying on the English. [*He coughs*] They asked me to work with the
English in order to find out their movements and report them right away
to some big personalities whose names I can't mention at the moment.
Of course I'm telling you this in confidence. No one should tell a soul.'

The sound of the demonstration grows louder.

HE: I'll say all that and they'll believe me. [*He points to the window*] They
are a good people, a people who wish everyone only good, who forget
quickly and like to have a good laugh.

*He approaches the window where the noise of the demonstration has
become even louder.*

HE: [*Pointing to the window*] The wave of people is approaching. I must
ride on the wave as it comes in so that I'm always on top of those
underneath. I'll make my voice the loudest ever, the very loudest.

*He seizes hold of the megaphone and hurries towards the window and joins
in the demonstration in a loud voice. The woman, meanwhile, slowly
lowers her arms and talks with exaggerated movements of her mouth; her
voice is not heard against his loud voice and the noise of the demonstration
which is calling out its slogans.*

HE: Long may Egypt live free! Long live the Egyptian people to vanquish
their invaders! Long live the national revolution of Egypt! Long live
Gamal Abdul Nasser! Down with tyrannical imperialism! To hell with
England! [*He crosses the room and hurries towards the door, still*

cheering. As he passes by the woman he shouts] Long live the people's resistance! Long live Socialism!

He hurries out through the door of the room, still cheering. The light in the room goes out as he makes his exit, then the ceiling light goes out too. The woman remains standing in the circle of light from the desk lamp, her hair having turned completely white. The noise of the demonstration in the street, led by Zainati, can be heard. The magic lantern shows the words 'The End' on the back wall, after which the light from the desk lamp goes out.

CURTAIN

The Trap

Alfred Farag

The Trap *by Alfred Farag*

Characters

THE OMDA, *Head of village*
GOUDA, *The Omda's guard*
THE HYENA, *A criminal on the run from the police*
VARIOUS WOMEN, PEASANTS AND GUARDS

The Place: *An outlying village in Upper Egypt*
The Time: *A winter's night*

Set: *A guest room in* THE OMDA's *house. To the right is a door leading to the outside, with a window opposite. To the left is a door leading into the interior of the house, and beside it, to the back of the stage, is an earthenware heating-stove, alongside which sits* THE OMDA. *There is a knocking at the door.* THE OMDA *turns round.* GOUDA *pushes the door open from the outside and enters.*

OMDA: Close the door, Gouda.
GOUDA: Heavens, it's so cold it dries up one's bones.
OMDA: Did you meet up with him?
GOUDA: Yes.
OMDA: Where he is?
GOUDA: Yes.
OMDA: You told him?
GOUDA: He told me he'd be coming at midnight.
OMDA: And the signal?
GOUDA: He'll give a howl like a wolf's.
OMDA: Squat down here. [GOUDA *sits down on the ground and puts his rifle beside him*] How is he?
GOUDA: The Hyena's the same as ever. He's sitting around in the sugar-cane as happy as a king.
OMDA: Bring the lamp nearer.

GOUDA: [*Moves the kerosene lamp nearer*] He said to me, 'Why does the Omda want me tonight?'

OMDA: And you . . . don't you know why?

GOUDA: Though I follow you about night and day like your shadow, from the moment you entered the police station this evening you've somehow changed.

OMDA: That's right.

GOUDA: Did the new investigating officer say anything to you?

OMDA: [*Slowly*] He said a great deal.

GOUDA: Let him say what he likes . . . who dares inform against us?

OMDA: [*Meaningfully*] This officer's very tough, Gouda.

GOUDA: And the one before him was also tough.

OMDA: But this fellow's very rugged, my boy.

GOUDA: Let him do as he likes.

OMDA: No, be very careful.

GOUDA: [*Seizing hold of his rifle*] Have you got something on your mind, Omda?

OMDA: Yes, I have.

GOUDA: Tell me about it.

OMDA: The officer's got a five-hundred-pound reward from the government for anyone who'll lead him to the Hyena.

GOUDA: [*Jumping to his feet in disbelief*] Five hundred pounds?

OMDA: Informing against him is now worth five hundred pounds.

GOUDA: Five hundred pounds!

OMDA: It's a clever move.

GOUDA: The price of two feddans of land?

OMDA: It's ten feddans' production of sugar-cane.

GOUDA: The Hyena's now priced at five hundred pounds.

OMDA: They put out some written notices in the streets round the police station this evening.

GOUDA: Heavens! [*He sits down directly by* THE OMDA's *feet*]

OMDA: He's a very rugged officer.

GOUDA: And did he ask to see you so as to tell you this?

OMDA: [*Meaningfully*] He told me a great deal.

GOUDA: Such as?

OMDA: He told me he knows everything.

GOUDA: What's he know?

OMDA: He knows I've been hiding the Hyena for three years.

GOUDA: He was trying to catch you out.

OMDA: He said to me: 'You're hiding him in the sugar-cane to the south of the canal.' [*A moment of silence.* GOUDA *has grasped hold of his rifle and placed it in his lap*]

GOUDA: [*In a grave tone*] You didn't tell me, Omda.

OMDA: And that he killed that irrigation engineer.

GOUDA: Is that so?

OMDA: He said to me: 'You're going half and half with the Hyena in the protection money.'

GOUDA: You didn't tell me about it earlier this evening.

OMDA: Why should I?

GOUDA: I'd have put him on the train to Sohag this very evening.

OMDA: The government's keeping an eye on all the trains.

GOUDA: We could take him by the mountain road.

OMDA: And if they caught up with him in Sohag?

GOUDA: My in-laws are a really tough lot down there.

OMDA: The five hundred pounds will be after him wherever he goes . . . it's his destiny.

GOUDA: He's better off staying where he is.

OMDA: And if they find him?

GOUDA: They'll find the blue djinn before they find him.

OMDA: Five hundred pounds, Gouda.

GOUDA: And if someone does inform against him, the sugar-cane's thick enough . . . let them search for him as long as they like.

OMDA: And if they bring along dogs?

GOUDA: They'll not take the Hyena alive.

OMDA: But if they do take him alive?

GOUDA: They'll have a fierce animal on their hands.

OMDA: And if they beat him and break his bones?

GOUDA: He'll not talk.

OMDA: And if they burn him with irons?

GOUDA: [*In a deliberate tone*] Would they burn him with irons?

OMDA: Wasn't the engineer he killed a government official and won't the government avenge their own?

GOUDA: Stones would talk before the Hyena does.

OMDA: And if the Hyena does talk?

GOUDA: He'll be putting his own head in the noose.

OMDA: And if they work on him and make him talk?

GOUDA: [*Affecting ignorance*] It's nothing to us if he does talk.

OMDA: Isn't it?

GOUDA: Is there anything on us?

OMDA: Didn't we have something to do with the engineer's death?

GOUDA: [*Surprised*] Oh that!

OMDA: Didn't we have something to do with the killing of Salama? . . . with the burning of Mansour's crops? And the northern patch of land? Haven't we got something to do with the protection money?

GOUDA: [*In alarm*] Hey, mind what you're saying, Omda. Walls have ears.

OMDA: The roads are watched and the five hundred pounds . . .

GOUDA: [*Catching on*] You're worried about someone in the village?

OMDA: Five hundred pounds would turn your own brother against you.

GOUDA: [*Feeling his way*] He'll be coming now and we can consult him.

OMDA: Let's consult among ourselves first.

GOUDA: You're a clever man, Omda. Speak.

OMDA: Put a couple of corncobs on the fire.

GOUDA: [*Puts two corncobs onto the fire and blows at it*] What do you suggest we do?

OMDA: [*With quiet determination*] We'll kill him.

GOUDA: [*Disturbed and mystified*] What did you say, Omda?

OMDA: We'll kill him.

GOUDA: [*Fumbling*] The officer?

OMDA: [*In a peremptory tone*] The Hyena.

GOUDA: [*As though stung by a scorpion*] What did you say?

OMDA: [*Sharply*] We'll kill the Hyena.

GOUDA: [*Recovering from the shock*] Don't say such a thing, Omda.

OMDA: The noose is round your neck.

GOUDA: [*Disapprovingly*] Has it come to this?

OMDA: Shut up, boy.

GOUDA: Betrayal's dirty.

OMDA: The hangman's noose is dirtier.

GOUDA: We all have to die, but one's honour is precious.

OMDA: Honour, boy?

GOUDA: Yes, honour.

OMDA: And you're talking about honour, guard?

GOUDA: I've stolen, I've done people harm, but betrayal's shameful, Omda.

OMDA: And what about betraying your badge of office, boy?

GOUDA: I'm Gouda Saafan. Here's my badge of office! [*He throws off his tarboosh and begins to take off his overcoat*] I'm Gouda Saafan!

OMDA: And your betrayal of Salama when you persuaded him to go into the fields with you for the Hyena to shoot him?

GOUDA: Salama's another question. He didn't put his trust in me. All the way he was looking sideways at me. If only he'd trusted me, I'd have brought him back safe.

OMDA: And the betrayal of the engineer? Didn't I appoint you as his guard and he had such trust in you that you smuggled the Hyena right into his house?

GOUDA: [*Still finding the matter distasteful*] Betrayal's shameful, Omda.

OMDA: And when our children cry and our spirits are broken in the police station and in the court, and we're dragged through the mud and end up on the gallows . . . isn't that shameful?

GOUDA: [*Still protesting*] Would that you hadn't lived and hadn't come to this, Gouda.

OMDA: [*His voice becomes gentler, like someone moving round his adversary in a cautious manoeuvre in which he seeks out his point of weakness*] And if the Hyena falls, will he cover up for us?

GOUDA: [*Eagerly defending his position*] In the same way as we've covered up for him he'll cover up for us.

OMDA: They'll torment him; like a wolf in a trap.

GOUDA: He'll see it out.

OMDA: He'll take it hard being alone in the dock and he'll take it hard our washing our hands of him with the government. He'll take it hard being cast out like a dog while you're sitting happily among your children.

GOUDA: We treated him well in the past.

OMDA: And then they'll dangle the hangman's noose in front of him . . . they'll scare the wits out of him.

GOUDA: A real man can take adversity.

OMDA: And then they'll tempt him.

GOUDA: What will they tempt him with?

OMDA: If you informed on the Omda and Gouda you'd escape with your neck.

GOUDA: [*In terror*] They'll tempt him?

OMDA: He's a very rugged officer.

GOUDA: And why should he believe them?

OMDA: He might believe them.

GOUDA: Would he be fooled?

OMDA: When a man becomes frightened he betrays.

GOUDA: [*Unbelieving*] He'd be tempted?

OMDA: A murderer! A brigand! A robber! Such a man can be hired against his own brother.

GOUDA: We know from experience the Hyena's a real man, Omda.

OMDA: A real man doesn't shoot someone in the dark . . . he doesn't kill treacherously, hiding behind somebody else.

GOUDA: But I shot someone in the dark.

OMDA: [*Bringing him round gradually*] That was for a purpose.

GOUDA: And we achieved the purpose.

OMDA: And tonight you'll shoot in order to save your neck. Either you shoot him or he'll drag you on to the gallows with him . . . and I'll be following behind.

GOUDA: [*Bewildered and feeling trapped*] I'm helpless, Omda.

OMDA: And your children are more helpless, my boy.

GOUDA: [*Like someone preparing himself against a danger*] My children?

OMDA: Hunger has already torn at their bellies and you can't find the price of a smoke, and the boy's eyes are burning with disease and you don't have the money to pay the district doctor's fee. You're no better than animal dung, without a feddan of land or somewhere to lay your head, and those miserable children of yours will be miserable orphans, with their father kicking out on the end of a rope.

GOUDA: Heavens! Would that you had no ears to hear with, Gouda.

OMDA: And the five hundred pounds will be made merry with by some informer you wouldn't hire for an onion. If every creature takes what is destined for him, then our children are more deserving of the money . . . and to hell with the hangman.

GOUDA: I broke the loaf of bread with my own hand, laid out the salt in my palm and then you dipped into it and then the Hyena and then I dipped into it.

OMDA: 'A good brain is a blessing' . . . they said it long ago.

GOUDA: I've got no brain left in my head.

OMDA: The man with brains buys what's good for him.

GOUDA: [*Like one reading destiny*] With the blood of his brother.

OMDA: The Hyena's blood is already spilt.

GOUDA: I wished he'd died a natural death.

OMDA: The government knows where he is . . . It's just a question of time. His blood is already spilt . . . he's finished.

GOUDA: [*Still faint-hearted*] Find a way out for us, Omda.

OMDA: If we don't bury our secret which is in his heart, the government will search us out.

GOUDA: Is that so?

OMDA: His carcase is worth five hundred pounds . . . two hundred and fifty pounds for you and two hundred and fifty for me.

GOUDA: The guilt of doing him in is more costly to us than that.

OMDA: The guilt will be on the police station which has spilt his blood, my boy. It's the officer who has really killed him, and it's we who're going to save him from the going-over he'll have during the interrogation and at the trial.

GOUDA: If it weren't for the five hundred pounds I'd be only too happy to believe you, Omda.

OMDA: Will the five hundred pounds burn you?

GOUDA: I'm saving my neck at the price of my friend's . . . fine. But to take money as the price of my friend I can't stomach.

OMDA: It's legitimate money, Gouda.

GOUDA: Legitimate?

OMDA: The Sheikh of the mosque will tell you so.

GOUDA: [*He is bewildered and stutters; then opens his eyes in astonishment*] Amazing!!

OMDA: It's all right so long as it comes from the government . . . and legitimately too. [*Quoting the proverb*] Goha is more deserving of the meat of his own ox.

GOUDA: Amazing!

OMDA: Aren't you the government guard? All you'll have done is to have killed a criminal.'

GOUDA: Will everyone say that?

OMDA: The people will be happy to be rid of his mischief.

GOUDA: Heavens!

OMDA: Gouda my boy . . . be of firm heart, boy.

GOUDA: [*Gazing round the guest room like someone looking for a refuge*] My heart tells me something, Omda.

OMDA: What's it tell you?

GOUDA: [*Looking him in the face*] And how will you be able to trust me after I've sold my friend for two hundred and fifty pounds, legitimately?

OMDA: I trust you like my own finger.

GOUDA: And the Hyena had the same trust in me. Correct?

OMDA: It's I who've urged you on to kill him, boy.

GOUDA: [*Staring at him searchingly*] Give me the two hundred and fifty pounds beforehand.

OMDA: [*Angrily*] Don't you trust me, boy?

GOUDA: It's you who'll be getting the five hundred pounds. Correct?

OMDA: Yes, I'll be getting the money.

GOUDA: And I?

OMDA: You get half and I get half.

GOUDA: And how can I trust you after this ill-fated hour, Omda?

OMDA: Are you going against me?

GOUDA: Five hundred pounds is a lot of money . . . it makes me tremble.

OMDA: You want to get it before you do the job?

GOUDA: You're strange. Don't you trust me, Omda?

OMDA: You've gone mad, boy.

GOUDA: You're right . . . my mind's in a whirl. My eyes look and don't see.

OMDA: Why, Gouda?

GOUDA: From the moment you said to me 'The man with brains buys what's good for him.'

OMDA: Your interest is the same as mine, and we're buying it half and half.

GOUDA: You kill him, Omda.

OMDA: [*Irritated*] If I killed him you wouldn't get a thing.

GOUDA: Why though? If I kill him it's half and half, and if you kill him . . .

OMDA: [*Interrupting him*] Weren't you always for hire for five pounds . . . or do you think I don't remember?

GOUDA: This whole village doesn't have five hundred pounds. Has the Devil come to join us, Omda?

OMDA: You mean to say the two hundred and fifty pounds will turn me against you?

GOUDA: God knows.

OMDA: Don't we each hold a secret which would lead to the gallows?

GOUDA: Meaning what?

OMDA: Meaning that I'll either keep you quiet with two hundred and fifty pounds or I'll kill you.

GOUDA: You kill me?

OMDA: If I didn't give you your share, then perhaps you'd feel badly done by and you'd lose your head and turn against me.

GOUDA: Ah . . .

OMDA: Have you got it?

GOUDA: [*Picking up the rifle. Silence*] So there's no trust any more?

OMDA: This is trust . . . your secret which is with me and my secret which is with you.

GOUDA: That's correct.

OMDA: You've come to your senses?

GOUDA: It's for you to give the orders, Omda.

OMDA: Thanks be to God. You had me worried, boy.

GOUDA: [*In a deep voice mingled with sadness*] I'll put your mind at rest, Omda.

OMDA: [*Taking on a sudden joyous energy*] Now the Hyena's coming. Directly you hear his wolf's howl, hide yourself behind the door. I'll stay in the middle of the guest room. You open the door a bit and let him in. And right away let him have a shot . . . and don't miss, boy.

GOUDA: And then?

OMDA: And then we'll inform the police station and they'll come and find him fallen with his own weapon beside him. We'll say he attacked us in the guest room.

GOUDA: They'll believe it?

OMDA: They'll put out the flags and every officer will take a pip, and nobody'll know a thing.

GOUDA: A proper trap, Omda.

OMDA: I've planned it step by step. [*He rubs his hands happily*]

GOUDA: You're a clever man, Omda.

OMDA: Shshsh . . . [*The sound of a wolf's howling. They both listen carefully. Tension*] Answer him.

GOUDA *answers him with a similar howl. At a sign from* THE OMDA *he hides behind the door and opens it a little, while* THE OMDA *gets ready in the centre of the guest room to receive* THE HYENA. *A moment of silence. The door opens from outside and* THE HYENA *passes through it. He hesitates. He gives a glance of doubt . . . the strange intuition of people on the run at the approach of danger.*

THE HYENA: [*In a sudden resonant voice: life has trained him to employ the element of surprise in dangerous circumstances*] What are you standing like that for, Omda?

OMDA: [*Confused and embarrassed*] Come in. Come in. [*He advances a step by way of tempting him to enter, though his voice almost betrays him*] Come in. Welcome.

THE HYENA: [*He is still examining the position and his grip has tightened on his rifle. He advances a step to find out what is around him. His voice is suspicious and harsh*] Are you going to betray me, Omda?

OMDA: [*His voice trembles*] Welcome . . . come in.

THE HYENA: [*He is now more aware of what is happening and his*

determination has strengthened] So that's it? [*He rushes towards* THE
OMDA, *firmly grasping the rifle*]

OMDA: Shoot, boy!

There is a shot. It misses. GOUDA *trembles and* THE HYENA *changes
direction and moves towards him with his huge lithe body. There is a
second shot from* GOUDA's *rifle, and a look of astonishment crosses*
THE HYENA's *face as the bullet penetrates his body.*

OMDA: Finish him off, Gouda.

GOUDA *is at the peak of his excitement. His rifle is aimed at the centre of
the guest room.* THE HYENA *strives to keep hold of his rifle which he has
aimed at* GOUDA, *while* GOUDA's *rifle is aimed at* THE OMDA.

OMDA: [*Gasping for breath*] Well done, Gouda! Again! [*He wakes up to the
situation, seeing that Gouda's rifle is aimed at him. He is suddenly very
frightened*] No, Gouda!

Two shots. The three stagger. GOUDA's *rifle has fallen: he has been hit but
is still on his feet. The other two fall down. Women, peasants and guards
rush into the guest room. There is much shouting and confusion.*

GOUDA: Are they dead? Speak. Are they dead?

THE GUARD: Get the women out, guard . . . no one at all must stay here.

GOUDA: Are they dead?!

GUARD: God rest their souls.

GOUDA: [*Falling on his knees with a sigh of relief*] Tell the head guard to
inform the police station that I killed the Hyena. It's I who've earned the
reward. He was struggling with the Omda and I fired two bullets at him.
One hit the Omda by mistake.

GUARD: You can rest now. Rest. [*He moves away*]

GOUDA: [*Aside*] You told me, Omda: there's no more trust. The man with
brains buys what's good for him. A scorpion has died by its own
poison.

CURTAIN

Marital Bliss

Abdel-Moneim Selim

Marital Bliss *by Abdel-Moneim Selim*

Cast

HUSBAND

WIFE

The Place: *A flat in Cairo*
The Time: *The present*

Set: *It is to be noted, first of all, that 'right' here means 'right' in relation to the audience and that 'left' is 'left' in relation to the audience.*

A spacious room with two doors at the back: a door on the right and a door on the left. A large-sized bed is placed between these two doors; it lies head forwards and extends to approximately half the stage. There is a small table, which is used for meals, near the middle of the stage, two chairs and an armchair. On the right is a small wardrobe, a television set, and a small mirror on the wall. On the left is a gramophone, a small library and a telephone.

When the curtain rises the television set is on, the volume high. The wife is sitting watching the television attentively, while at the same time the husband is engrossed in listening to one of Beethoven's Quartets on the gramophone. The sound of the music is also so loud that in the end a state of distortion is reached, neither the wife being able to concentrate on the programme nor the husband on the music.

HUSBAND AND WIFE: [*Both together, shouting*] It's absolutely impossible.
HUSBAND: I can't hear a thing.
WIFE: And I too can neither hear nor watch.
HUSBAND: Stop that row. [*Pointing to the television*]
WIFE: You stop your own row. [*Pointing to the record-player*]
HUSBAND: I'm free to listen to whatever I want to.
WIFE: And I'm free to watch whatever I want to.

The husband rushes up to the television set and turns it off, while simultaneously the wife goes and turns off the record-player.

HUSBAND AND WIFE: [*Together*] God help us.
HUSBAND: Please . . . do please give me the chance of listening to my record.
WIFE: And you give me the chance of watching my programme.
HUSBAND: I only bought the record today.
WIFE: The record can wait; the television programme can't.

She goes to the television set and turns it on, while he rushes to the record-player. We hear a medley of sounds. Both the husband and wife try to pretend not to be paying any attention to the other, but they in fact do so at a cost to their nerves. Thus, after a while, they explode simultaneously.

HUSBAND AND WIFE: [*Together*] It's absolutely impossible.
HUSBAND: [*Calmly*] Impossible. No, it's utterly impossible. Like this life's impossible.

He goes to the television set and turns it off. The wife has turned off the record-player.

WIFE: Now you can explain to me why it is you don't want me to watch the programme.
HUSBAND: Who's stopping who?
WIFE: That's a stupid question. The matter's perfectly obvious . . . television programmes are something you can't control . . . they're exactly like radio programmes . . . while record-players and tape-recorders are things you can control.
HUSBAND: Look here, Sana . . . the fact of the matter is, it's got nothing to do with tape-recorders, television sets or record-players. It has to do with our very life. Our life together has become impossible.
WIFE: Because of the television?
HUSBAND: Because of the television and other things.
WIFE: What are you trying to say?
HUSBAND: I'm saying to you that . . . I don't want to say anything. Let's close the subject now. [*Calmly*] What's for food? Have you eaten?
WIFE: I had a snack . . . I thought you'd be late as usual.

HUSBAND: What do you mean 'as usual'? You always take it for granted I must be late.

WIFE: If you'd only told me . . .

HUSBAND: If you'd only asked me.

WIFE: If I had asked you there'd only have been a quarrel.

HUSBAND: Because you don't ask like a wife should, but like a public prosecutor . . . as though you were starting a cross-examination.

WIFE: What can I do about it, it's just my manner of talking, my manner of asking questions?

HUSBAND: One should change one's manner in accordance with the situation. It's silly always to behave in the same way. Look how the other day when you asked your friend Salwa where she was going to after the cinema . . . what did she say to you? Answer me. Didn't she say 'you're spying on me'? Now that's exactly what you do with me.

WIFE: But I've never spied on you, and I've never intended to indicate by anything I've said that I was spying on you.

HUSBAND: Intentions are one thing and what actually happens another.

WIFE: So what's the solution now?

HUSBAND: The solution is that I should have something to eat. What is there?

WIFE: Didn't I tell you I'd be making rice with vermicelli and sugar . . .

HUSBAND: [*Raising his face and hands skywards in despair*] Heaven help us!

WIFE: What?

HUSBAND: How many years have we been married?

WIFE: What?

HUSBAND: [*Shouting*] Answer me!

WIFE: Three . . . four.

HUSBAND: Four whole long years, i.e. more than a thousand days, and every day I've been telling you I don't like rice. Every day I've been telling you this three times a day . . . three times . . . once with every meal. That's to say I've told you a million times and yet you've still made rice.

WIFE: But vermicelli can never be eaten without rice.

HUSBAND: Who said so?

WIFE: I've never cooked rice without vermicelli.

HUSBAND: [*Calmly*] You mean vermicelli without rice.

WIFE: Yes.

HUSBAND: [*Calmly*] But I don't like rice, so what's the solution?

WIFE: Make an effort and eat rice with vermicelli.

HUSBAND: Why should I make an effort?

WIFE: Because I've cooked it.

HUSBAND: And why didn't you cook me vermicelli without rice?

WIFE: You mean to say I should cook twice?

HUSBAND: Why not?

WIFE: It's not reasonable I should cook twice a day.

HUSBAND: [*Calmly*] Why? Explain to me why. At the office I carry out a routine job every day and yet I've never got fed up with it. At least when you're cooking you're not doing something routine . . . you're creating something new.

WIFE: But that new thing will soon become routine.

HUSBAND: [*Calmly*] My dear woman, let's not bring philosophy into it. The matter is exceedingly clear . . . you like rice; you can't sit down to a meal without having rice; while I don't like rice; can't eat anything with rice in it. The solution is therefore exceedingly simple: you cook a helping of rice for yourself but no helping of rice for me. Instead you cook me something else, something I like.

HUSBAND: Like blancmange.

WIFE: I don't like it.

HUSBAND: And I love it. Just for once I'd like to have blancmange for a sweet.

WIFE: [*In amazement*] Just for once! What do you think you had yesterday? Wasn't it blancmange? And the day before and the day before that . . .

HUSBAND: [*Continuing, heedless of having interrupted her*] Why don't you make blancmange? Why do you deprive me of blancmange?

WIFE: [*Shouting*] I've deprived you? I make it for you every day.

HUSBAND: [*Continuing, heedless of having interrupted her*] Have I deprived you of eating rice? Just as you make something for yourself, make something . . .

WIFE: [*Irritably*] Seeing that you don't want to listen to what I say, seeing that you won't recognise what I do, let me tell you that it's out of the question for me to cook something for you every day that's different from what I'm cooking for myself.

HUSBAND: I asked you to do this? Anyway, why not? Tell me why not. Quite frankly, eating's a very personal matter. As the saying goes, every man to his taste. For years now I haven't been eating to my taste; I've been eating to your taste. That's not fair, it's no life.

WIFE: Please calm down.

HUSBAND: No, the matter must be resolved. It must be resolved today . . . right now.

WIFE: What do you want then?

HUSBAND: I want to make out a programme for my eating.

WIFE: All right, but eat first.

HUSBAND: [*In surprise and at a loss*] Rice with vermicelli. [*Shouting*] I won't eat rice with vermicelli, never ever. I shan't have dinner, I shan't have dinner for as long as I live . . what more do you want?

WIFE: All right, all right.

HUSBAND: Beginning from today . . . beginning from tomorrow you must make me my own food. You must make me the food I like, the food I'm fond of, the food I was brought up on for thirty years at home before I got married. Do you understand? From today . . . from tomorrow, everything must change. [*Pauses*] I can't bear any food with sauce.

WIFE: You mean you don't want me to cook any food with sauce?

HUSBAND: Cook for yourself as you like, but not for me.

WIFE: What will you eat then?

HUSBAND: Make me every day some grilled meat, fried meat . . . I want dry things.

WIFE: You know that food with sauces can be used twice . . . it's more economical.

HUSBAND: You can eat it twice . . . three or four times, just as you like, but not for me.

WIFE: You know what this means, don't you?

HUSBAND: What?

WIFE: This means that the household budget will be doubled.

HUSBAND: It doesn't matter. Why do I work? What am I earning money for? [*He answers his own question calmly*] In order to do what I want to, in order to choose what I like.

WIFE: Wouldn't it be better if we were to save and get ourselves another room instead of being cooped up in one room like this?

HUSBAND: You want me to get furniture for a second room? All right. But where do we get a second room from? Please think within the limits of the possibilities that exist.

WIFE: You too must think within the limits of such possibilities.

HUSBAND: I'm prepared not to go out in the evening, to give up smoking, to do everything possible in order that I may eat what I want.

WIFE: What else do you want?

HUSBAND: You know that for me sauces are out.

WIFE: All right, but then how do you want your vegetables cooked?

HUSBAND: Boiled.

WIFE: People only eat them boiled when they're ill.

HUSBAND: Who said so? Throughout the whole of the world people eat vegetables boiled, so all of them are therefore ill.

WIFE: I'm not talking about people abroad.

HUSBAND: [*His patience exhausted*] I'm ill . . . no, not ill . . . I've died. When I say I want to eat boiled things, I mean boiled. A piece of grilled meat with a few boiled vegetables and a small piece of bread, followed by an orange, a banana, an apple, some blancmange.

WIFE: [*Derisively*] Foreigners' food.

HUSBAND: [*As though he hasn't heard her*] That's the food I want.

WIFE: It's just as though we were living in two separate houses.

HUSBAND: How's that? We're eating at one table, sleeping in one bed.

WIFE: [*Interrupting and regretful*] But each will have his own dish, and each dish will contain different food.

HUSBAND: Listen, Sana . . .

WIFE: [*Interrupting*] There's no point in talking now. What shall I bring you to eat?

HUSBAND: I told you I'll have nothing to do with rice with vermicelli.

WIFE: That's it, then . . . I'll eat the rice with vermicelli.

HUSBAND: Fine.

WIFE: There's cheese and honey and there's also lentil soup. You like lentil soup.

HUSBAND: Yes, I like lentil soup, but I also want some cheese and honey.

WIFE: Certainly.

She goes out. He puts on a gramophone record, sets it going and seats himself in the armchair, reading the paper. The wife enters and puts the dish of rice and vermicelli on the table.

WIFE: What's the news in the paper today? [*He doesn't reply*] Why don't you answer?

HUSBAND: Are you getting the food or do you want to hear the news?

WIFE: Tell me the news and then I'll bring it.

HUSBAND: When I've finished reading the paper, then you can go ahead and read it.

WIFE: In short, I shall never read the paper.

HUSBAND: [*In astonishment*] How's that?

WIFE: Because your lordship never lets go of the newspaper. You even read it in bed before you go to sleep. Actually, by rights, you should have read the paper by now.

HUSBAND: Why should I?

WIFE: The paper's been with you all day long at the office.

HUSBAND: So what?

WIFE: So you must have read it.

HUSBAND: My dear girl, office hours don't belong to me, they belong to the State, to the people. Do you want me to waste people's time reading the newspaper?

WIFE: If that's so, then why take it with you?

HUSBAND: Would you be so good as to tell me where the food is?

WIFE: At least tell me the most interesting news and then I'll bring it.

HUSBAND: Not again!

WIFE: The best solution is for us to have two papers a day . . . you can take one to work with you and leave one at home for me to read.

HUSBAND: [*As though he has come across a wonderful solution*] An excellent idea!

WIFE: That's it then . . . I'll put it into effect as from tomorrow.

She goes out to bring the rest of the food. He follows her out with his eyes, then gives a long sigh and goes back to reading the paper. The music continues. The wife enters with a tray on which are four dishes. The dish of rice and vermicelli is already in front of her on the table. She puts down the four dishes in front of her husband: one contains lentil soup, another a piece of cheese, a third some honey, and the fourth bread.

WIFE: It's ready.

He puts the newspaper aside and goes over to the gramophone and turns down the volume. They sit down. The wife crosses her legs. They begin to eat. Moments pass.

HUSBAND: Do you mind?

WIFE: What?

HUSBAND: Your legs.

WIFE: What's wrong with them?

HUSBAND: I want to stretch mine out.

WIFE: And I want to have mine crossed.

HUSBAND: What's the solution?

WIFE: I can't sit down without crossing my legs.

HUSBAND: And I can't sit down unless I can stretch one out on top of the other.

WIFE: And what's stopping you?

HUSBAND: Your legs.

WIFE: This is the way I find most comfortable for sitting.

HUSBAND: And this is exactly the way I find most comfortable for sitting.

WIFE: You are of course interested in my comfort. [*He doesn't reply*] If you're interested in my comfort, then you must sacrifice your own a bit.

HUSBAND: A bit? It wouldn't matter if it was a bit. I'm sacrificing a great deal. My dear girl, I've been suffering from this business for four years. For four whole years I've been tortured. For four whole years I've felt oppressed. For four years I haven't been able to enjoy the space under the table.

WIFE: And what's made you bring up this subject now?

HUSBAND: I bring it up every day but it's no use. You're unable to appreciate my position.

WIFE: Your position?

HUSBAND: [*With determination*] Yes . . . the position of my legs.

WIFE: If I'd ever known you minded so much, things would never have developed in this way.

HUSBAND: [*Fearfully*] Developed?

WIFE: Naturally I can't change the way I sit. For four years I've been sitting like this. For four years I've been sitting with my legs crossed. For four years I haven't changed the way I sit. It isn't only four years either . . . my whole life I've been used to sitting like this when I'm at home.

HUSBAND: [*Calmly*] So what's the solution now?

WIFE: There's no solution . . . we just go on.

HUSBAND: Impossible.

WIFE: Listen, why do you imagine I oppose you? In my view the question is simply that I share with you the space under the table. Marriage is a partnership, isn't it?

HUSBAND: [*As though thinking*] Yes, marriage is a partnership. I want to share the space with you. Give me my share of the space so that I can feel we really are a partnership. [*Silence*] Yes?

WIFE: [*Calmly*] You really aren't being fair.

HUSBAND: [*In astonishment*] I?

WIFE: Yes, you . . . and I'll prove to you here and now that you're not being fair. [*Quickly*] You do of course agree with me that fairness is the basis of everything?

HUSBAND: [*Cautiously*] And one's right too.

WIFE: I agree: fairness and one's rights. Now, first of all, I'll show you how little I care about my own rights; and secondly, that I'm being fair.

HUSBAND: How's that?

WIFE: Look at the table. [*She points at the food*]

HUSBAND: Yes.

WIFE: How many dishes are there on the table?

HUSBAND: What are you getting at?

WIFE: Answer me first.

HUSBAND: Three . . . four.

WIFE: How many exactly?

HUSBAND: A dish for the bread, another for the cheese, a dish for the honey, another for the lentil soup, and a dish of rice and vermicelli . . . that's to say five dishes.

WIFE: Out of those five dishes . . . how many are mine and how many are yours?

HUSBAND: What are you getting at?

WIFE: Answer, please.

HUSBAND: One dish is yours and the rest are for me. So – is there anything wrong in that?

WIFE: Not at all. There's nothing wrong. You and I own this table . . . we own its surface and we own the space underneath it. As you want us to share the space under the table, so I must share its surface with you.

HUSBAND: [*Cautiously*] I don't understand.

WIFE: I've got a share in the surface, a share equal to exactly half the table, yet you with your four dishes are trespassing on my part.

HUSBAND: But you are losing nothing because you don't need more than one dish.

WIFE: I don't care . . . you're trespassing on my share of the surface and you've been trespassing on it for four years. Four whole years, and yet I've never before permitted myself to bring up the matter and discuss it with you.

HUSBAND: So that's why you trespassed on the space underneath?

WIFE: Didn't I have to make up for what I'd lost on the surface? At least I should sit in comfort.

HUSBAND: [*Severely*] Listen here, I shall not allow this situation to go on for ever. This question must be resolved now.

WIFE: It can't possibly be resolved.

HUSBAND: Why not?

WIFE: Firstly, because I by nature always use one dish . . . I put into it the rice and the vegetables, the meat and the salad. You, however, like to have in front of you as many dishes as you have things to eat, which means that for the whole of your life you'll go on trespassing on my share of the surface . . .

HUSBAND: [*Completing what she is saying*] . . . and you'll go on trespassing for the whole of your life on my share of the space which is under the surface.

WIFE: Why do you call it trespass?

HUSBAND: [*Shouting*] This situation must end.

WIFE: Fine, but just don't shout.

HUSBAND: But . . .

WIFE: What?

HUSBAND: I've found it.

WIFE: You've found what?

HUSBAND: [*Joyfully*] I've found the solution.

WIFE: What's the solution?

HUSBAND: [*Joyfully*] Listen here . . . [*As though recollecting some mathematical formula or as though he's a teacher explaining something*] . . . you must sit and put one leg over another, while I must sit and stretch both my legs out to the fullest extent . . . isn't that so?

WIFE: H'm.

HUSBAND: [*In the same tone*] I can't stretch my legs out to the fullest extent because your legs are in the way.

WIFE: H'm.

HUSBAND: [*In the same tone*] If you put your legs down, and I stretch out mine, I'd be comfortable and you'd be uncomfortable.

WIFE: Quite.

HUSBAND: And if you don't put your legs down, I won't be able to stretch mine out. You'll be comfortable and I'll be uncomfortable . . .

WIFE: H'm.

HUSBAND: [*As though solving some abstruse mathematical problem . . . precisely and calmly*] If there were another table the result would be that you could sit as you liked and I could sit as I liked . . it means we'd both be comfortable.

WIFE: [*Half-sadly*] A second table.

HUSBAND: Yes, a second table.

WIFE: It means that each would be sitting at a table on his own.

HUSBAND: So long as we can both be comfortable that way, why not? It's a very brilliant idea. . . how is it we never thought of it before? [*He lifts up the telephone receiver*] Hullo . . . yes . . . a second table . . . the same size as the one we've got. [*Replaces the receiver*]

WIFE: This means that I'll be cleaning two tables instead of one.

HUSBAND: Who said so? As we've said, marriage is a partnership . . . a company.

WIFE: Meaning what?

HUSBAND: Meaning that each cleans his own table; each is responsible for his table. This is how it should be. Not only that . . . the right thing is that each should wash the dishes he uses.

WIFE: [*Tenderly*] Fancy, Ahmed, your thinking like that, thinking that you shouldn't tire me . . . you're the best man in the world.

HUSBAND: And you're the best woman in the world.

They exchange loud kisses. Directly the kissing ends a man enters carrying a table of exactly the same size as the first.

HUSBAND: Here's the table, it's arrived. Wait . . . yes, put it here.

WIFE: But it's not right there.

HUSBAND: We'll find a way later on. [*To the man*] Thanks. [*The man leaves*] Now, then, let's think about where we'll put it. What do you think about putting it like this?

He puts the table in front of the other in such a way that when he sits down his wife is sitting in front of him, which means that when he stretches out his feet his wife's legs are still in the way. He seats himself.

WIFE: Sit down like that, then.

HUSBAND: What do you think?

WIFE: Your legs.

HUSBAND: What about them?

WIFE: They come right up to where I am.

HUSBAND: H'm, it won't do placed like that. What do you think about putting it like this? [*He brings it close alongside the other one so that the two tables together form one long one, with her sitting in the middle, while he sits to one side]* H'm, sit down like this so we can see. [*They sit down*]

WIFE: Even so . . .

HUSBAND: Even so what?

WIFE: Even so your legs reach to where I am. You're forgetting that the root of the problem is that you stretch out your legs to the full.

HUSBAND: [*Correcting her*] I stretch my legs out to the full and you cross yours.

WIFE: The important thing is: what are we going to do now?

HUSBAND: What do you think? Wait . . . [*He places the two tables alongside each other as in the first positioning so that there is a gap between them in which he places the two chairs . . . the point being that when they sit down they are back to back*] Sit like this. [*They sit down*]

HUSBAND AND WIFE: [*Together*] No, no, it's ridiculous. [*They stand up at the same moment*]

WIFE: And now what?

HUSBAND: I've an excellent idea. What d'you think about moving it over there? [*Pointing to the left-hand side of the stage, i.e. left-hand side in relation to the audience*] Wait. [*He takes up the table and puts it down where, when seated, he will be sitting sideways to the audience, while she, when seated, is placed in the same position, i.e., they are ultimately facing each other when seated. He sits down*] What do you think? . . . couldn't be better.

WIFE: But we're very far apart.

HUSBAND: [*Taking no notice of her objection*] This is the best solution. Let's see when you sit down. [*She sits down. Each is now to one side of the stage and they are facing each other*] What do you think? Now I can stretch my legs right out to the middle of the room [*Stretches out his legs*] . . . like so. And you too can stretch out your legs or cross them. It means that each of us can do what he likes with his legs. What do you think?

WIFE: It's really very comfortable.

HUSBAND: Let's eat then. [*He collects his plates, places them on his table, then sits down. They start on the food*] Do you know, Sana, marital problems can be solved with the utmost ease. I mean, did you honestly imagine we'd reach this important decision and settle our troubles so simply by merely buying a second table.

WIFE: It's a really stupendous idea.

HUSBAND: It's certainly true that there are married people with trivial difficulties of this sort. [*As though he has discovered something*] You know, Sana, through one's experiences one could write a book entitled 'How to solve your Marital Problems' . . . small and very trivial things.

WIFE: But they mess up things.

HUSBAND: Indeed.

WIFE: But, listen . . . don't come along in the end and make a fool of me.

HUSBAND: A fool of you?

WIFE: By saying to me 'Take away the plates, clean up the table for me.'

HUSBAND: No, no, no, of course not . . . and just to prove to you that I really meant what I said to you, I myself will clear away my plates.

WIFE: You've finished eating?

HUSBAND: That was the most delicious meal I've had ever since we got married. [*He gets up and carries off the plates, making his way towards the bed*]

WIFE: Do you know, Ahmed, what I was thinking? [*Suddenly she notices that he intends to put the plates beside the bed*] What are you doing?

HUSBAND: I'm showing you how it is that I'm responsible for my table and for my plates.

WIFE: But where are you taking them to?

HUSBAND: Here . . . [*Pointing to the floor beside the bed*]

WIFE: Where's here? . . . beside the bed?

HUSBAND: So what?

WIFE: That's impossible Ahmed . . . you must take the plates to the kitchen.

HUSBAND: Look here, you do as you like with your own plates but let me do as I like with mine . . . leave them on the table, put them beside the bed . . . on top of the bed.

WIFE: But they must be washed.

HUSBAND: I'll wash them.

WIFE: When?

HUSBAND: That, Sana, is a question you've got no right to ask. I shall wash them when I like, when I feel like it . . . or, alternatively, I'm free not to wash them. These plates are my responsibility, I'm free to do with them as I please.

WIFE: Yes, but if you were to leave them beside the bed they'd start to smell. You haven't got this room to yourself, you know.

HUSBAND: Rest assured that I'll make every effort to see the smell doesn't reach you.

WIFE: How?

HUSBAND: I'll think, and I won't tell you. I'll spare you them . . . I'll take them outside.

WIFE: Outside where?

HUSBAND: Into the kitchen of course.

WIFE: Into the kitchen of course. But you must still wash them up immediately.

HUSBAND: You mean to say that you'll wash your plate up immediately?

WIFE: Note that it's only one plate. Even if I were to put it off for half an hour, an hour, even a whole day, it wouldn't make such a smell as all yours.

HUSBAND: But I'm not in the mood to wash them now . . . I'll put them on the kitchen table and wash them up later.

WIFE: And now you'll be dirtying the kitchen table.

HUSBAND: [*As though discovering something*] I'll tell you something . . . [*Calmly*] What we've done here we'll do in the kitchen.

WIFE: Meaning what?

The husband lifts up the telephone receiver.

WIFE: What are you going to do?

HUSBAND: Hullo . . . yes . . . a kitchen table . . . a small one . . . at once . . . [*He replaces the receiver. We immediately hear a sound from outside indicating that the man has brought the table*] Come along . . . the table's arrived. [*They go out. We hear sounds of movement*]

HUSBAND: [*From outside*] No, it's better if you put it here . . . isn't that so?

WIFE: Fair enough. [*The husband enters and takes out the plates*]

HUSBAND: [*From outside*] And here, my dear girl, are the plates on my table.

The sound of the plates being put down; then silence. Then there is loud laughter and the two of them come on to the stage, each with an arm round the other's waist, happily in love; a kiss may be exchanged at each step.

WIFE: Good for you, Ahmed. I can't understand how we didn't know ages ago how to go about things so efficiently. [*She kisses him*]

HUSBAND: Just imagine, today we kissed more than we've done all the years we've been married. [*He kisses her*]

WIFE: You know, Ahmed, what I was thinking about?

HUSBAND: Yes?

WIFE: I was thinking . . . if in an instant we've been able to solve a very great problem that has been upsetting our life for so long, why don't we try to solve the rest of our problems in the same way?

HUSBAND: Meaning?

WIFE: Meaning, look how much we quarrel about this chair. [*She points to the armchair*]

HUSBAND: It's you who did the quarrelling.

WIFE: You were continually taking possession of it.

HUSBAND: I used to return from work tired and liked to sit down, sit down relaxed and comfortable.

WIFE: And I too, don't I go out and buy vegetables, and to buy meat and fruit and bread? Aren't I responsible for all the household requirements? . . . and I sweep and dust and cook and wash.

HUSBAND: You couldn't possibly get more tired than I do.

WIFE: Let's not quarrel about the chair now.

HUSBAND: It's you who brought the subject up.

WIFE: What I'd like to say is why don't we solve the business of the chair in the same way as we've solved the business of the table?

HUSBAND: [*Calmly, as though considering*] You mean we should buy another armchair?

WIFE: Why not?

HUSBAND: You know how much it costs?

WIFE: What's the value of money if we don't use it to solve our problems instead of losing our tempers and upsetting ourselves.

HUSBAND: Quite right, it's better to lose our money. [*Raising his voice*] A very remarkable idea! [*He kisses her and makes for the telephone*]

WIFE: Are you going to get it now?

HUSBAND: Certainly. Why not? . . . no time like the present. [*He lifts the receiver*] Hullo . . . an armchair . . . exactly like the one we've got . . . [*Asking*] The colour? Just a moment please. [*Asks his wife*] What colour shall we have it, Sana?

WIFE: That chair [*Pointing to the chair in the room*] you bought to suit your taste, the next chair is going to be mine. I want it orange-coloured.

HUSBAND: Orange? What sort of colour's that?

WIFE: That's how I want it. I like orange.

HUSBAND: Sana, you must appreciate that you haven't got this room to yourself. I'm still living with you. This means that every day . . . every hour . . . I'll be looking at this orange colour, a colour I've never liked.

WIFE: I'll find a way round it . . . just order it that colour.

HUSBAND: Tell me the way round it first.

WIFE: Rest assured I'll make it all right for you. I'll put a cover on it. Just order that colour . . . go on.

HUSBAND: [*Defeated, talks into the telephone*] Orange-coloured . . . yes, orange. Thanks. [*He replaces the receiver. There is a knock at the door. The chair has arrived. The wife goes and opens the door. The man enters carrying an armchair. He puts it on the floor*] Put it over there, please. [*Points to a far corner of the room*]

WIFE: No, I want it here. [*Points to a place in the middle of the room*]

During this conversation the man's gaze alternates between the two of them in astonishment.

HUSBAND: How, though, can we put it here? It'll crowd the room.

WIFE: Move your chair away a bit.

HUSBAND: Even if I were to move it away it would still be crowding the room. There you are my dear girl, just so you'll believe me. [*He places the chair on the left side*]

WIFE: Yes, that's fine like that. [*To the man*] Would you be so good as to put the chair here. [*Points to a place on the right from where she is able to watch the television. The man begins to move the chair to the place she has indicated*]

HUSBAND: How can it go there though? [*To the man*] Thanks, that'll be all. [*The man goes out*]

WIFE: Because of the television.

HUSBAND: What about the television?

WIFE: [*Her patience exhausted*] So that I'll be able to watch the television.

HUSBAND: Fine . . . and me?

WIFE: What about you?

HUSBAND: But I too sometimes like to watch television. How can I watch it from my chair if it's so far away?

WIFE: When you want to watch the television you can bring your chair closer.

HUSBAND: I'll be doing a weight-lifting performance, carrying the chair from here to there every day. It's absurd.

WIFE: Move your chair alongside mine now and then don't move it again.

HUSBAND: In short I must go on looking at television for evermore.

WIFE: But why look at it?

HUSBAND: Because I like to sit in the armchair, and if I've moved it alongside your chair and have sat down in it, your ladyship always switches on the television and the natural outcome is that I'll stay on in front of the television screen.

WIFE: And the solution?

HUSBAND: [*Striking himself on the forehead*] I really am an idiot.

WIFE: [*In astonishment*] An idiot?

HUSBAND: Of course, a real thundering idiot. [*He raises the receiver*]

WIFE: What are you going to do?

HUSBAND: [*Into the telephone*] Hullo . . . a 23-inch television.

WIFE: A television!

HUSBAND: It's necessary . . . and 23 inches.

WIFE: [*In astonishment*] 23!

HUSBAND: 24, if that's possible.

WIFE: Mine is 21.

HUSBAND: [*Into the telephone*] Right away now. [*Puts down the receiver*] Didn't we say what's the value of money if we don't use it to solve our problems?

WIFE: That's right.

HUSBAND: Why should we get annoyed and quarrel over something inane. You'll have television and I'll have television. What better arrangement! Let's be happy and enjoy life. [*They kiss each other. A knocking at the door. He goes to the door and opens it. A man enters carrying a television set*]

[*To the man*] Wait. [*Thinks.*] I tell you, put it here. [*Pointing to the left-hand side*] Yes . . . thanks. [*The man goes out*] Now I can sit in the chair like this [*He sits down*] and when there's a programme I'll sit comfortably and watch.

WIFE: And I too can do the same thing. [*She sits on her chair for a moment, then the two of them get up together and exchange a long kiss*]

HUSBAND: What else is there?

WIFE: The mirror.

HUSBAND: I don't understand.

WIFE: Aren't you asking what else there is?

HUSBAND: Yes.

WIFE: I'll tell you what else we'll do. The mirror. We'll now try to solve the problem of the mirror.

HUSBAND: [*Pointing to the mirror on the wall*] This mirror?

WIFE: Is there another one?

HUSBAND: What about it?

WIFE: Because there isn't another one. [*A pause*] Why don't we get one?

HUSBAND: [*Understanding*] What you mean is why don't we buy another one?

WIFE: All our life we've been quarrelling over it when we've been going out together. I'll be wanting to do my hair and you too will be wanting to do yours, and the result is we get in each other's way and quarrel.

HUSBAND: [*With conviction*] That's right.

WIFE: Why then don't we buy a second one?

HUSBAND: Right away . . . we'll get a second one. [*He lifts the receiver*] Hullo. Yes, a mirror. Yes, a mirror. A wall mirror. Quickly, please. [*He replaces the receiver. A knocking at the door. He goes to the door and opens it, then closes it and returns carrying a mirror*] Where, then, shall we put it? [*Looks towards the left-hand side*] There's no other place for it except here.

WIFE: Just wait.

HUSBAND: Eh?

WIFE: [*Goes up to him and takes hold of the mirror*] Let go of this mirror.

HUSBAND: Let go of it . . . why should I let go of it?

WIFE: I'll be taking this mirror.

HUSBAND: And me?

WIFE: You take my mirror.

HUSBAND: Why, though?

WIFE: You shouldn't be taking all the new things.

HUSBAND: What new things have I been taking? You've just taken the new armchair, while I had the old one.

WIFE: And the 23-inch television and this table, and the kitchen table? But more important is that I'm a woman and need the mirror more than you.

HUSBAND: That's it then. Calm down. We never stop quarrelling. I have in fact taken the new table and my 23 inch television set. You're certainly entitled to take the mirror. The question is of the utmost simplicity: go ahead and have it. Not only that but I'll also fix your mirror on the wall for you. [*He moves over to the right-hand side where the mirror is and takes it down from its place*] Here's the old mirror and we've taken it down. [*He picks up the new one*] Don't let a thing upset you . . . here's the new one. [*He hangs it up in place of the old one and moves away from it slightly, looking at himself in it*] What do you think of it? [*She goes up to him and kisses him*]

WIFE: Come along, let's hang up your mirror.

HUSBAND: [*As though recollecting something*] Ah! [*Carrying the old mirror, he goes to the left-hand side, where he hangs it up on the wall*] That's the most suitable place for it. Isn't that so?

WIFE: Exactly.

HUSBAND: [*Looking at himself in the mirror*] Do you know, my appearance here is changed.

WIFE: How's it changed?

HUSBAND: It seems to me that before when the mirror was over there . . . by you [*He points to where she is*] . . . I used to find I looked as though I was getting thinner and was in poor health. Now the situation's completely changed . . . I look a lot better here.

WIFE: The point is merely [*Pause*] a question of angle . . . the angle at which the mirror is placed.

HUSBAND: But it's the same angle.

WIFE: At my angle there's more light . . . in yours there's less.

HUSBAND: And what have lights and angles to do with it?

WIFE: Too little light always makes one look unwell.

HUSBAND: [*Calmly*] Maybe.

WIFE: The important thing is, we've achieved something.

HUSBAND: It seems to me that if we were to give it more thought we'd achieve what we want.

WIFE: What is it that we want?

HUSBAND: Marital happiness, and marital happiness cannot be achieved unless we get rid of marital problems. Our problems are obvious ones and the solving of them simple . . . it's in our own hands. If only every husband in the world were to sit down and come to an understanding with his wife, don't you honestly think they'd overcome their difficulties? Mutual understanding solves difficulties, mutual understanding is the basis of marital happiness.

WIFE: Certainly. Who would believe that in a matter of moments we've been able to solve problems that were threatening our marital life every day. At one time I was thinking I wouldn't be able to go on.

HUSBAND: You too?

WIFE: You too?

HUSBAND: We must do as you said, we must really try and make an effort to see what the other things are that are upsetting us. I'm convinced that by mutual understanding we'll solve them. [*Suddenly*] The tragedy is that our troubles were all over silly things. The human psyche is really very complicated.

WIFE: You know there's something very important you've forgotten.

HUSBAND: What's that?

WIFE: The wardrobe.

HUSBAND: What about the wardrobe?

WIFE: It's one of the problems we mustn't be afraid to face up to.

HUSBAND: Of course we must face up to it. What is there to be afraid of? I'll never be afraid. What about the wardrobe?

WIFE: Aren't you always complaining that because of your having so many suits and me so many dresses, the result is . . .

HUSBAND: [*Quickly*] . . . that my suits get squashed up and want ironing every day.

WIFE: And my dresses get crumpled and also want ironing every day. [*He walks in the direction of the telephone*] What are you going to do?

HUSBAND: [*Joyfully*] The solution's obvious. [*He lifts the receiver*] You're right . . . the quarrels we had about the collar of my coat which your dresses were crushing! . . . What quarrels we had because of my shirts and because of my ties! [*Into the telephone*] Hullo, yes . . . a wardrobe. Same size and dimensions. Exactly. [*He replaces the receiver and immediately a knocking is heard at the door. He goes to open it and a man enters carrying a light-weight wardrobe which he puts down in the middle of the room*] It doesn't make sense putting it here. I'll tell what . . . put it here. [*Indicating a corner alongside his mirror*]

WIFE: Which means that you'll be having the wardrobe for yourself.

HUSBAND: Why not?

WIFE: Then I'm to hang on to the old wardrobe and you're to have the new one!

HUSBAND: It's you who bought the old wardrobe with the rest of the furniture.

WIFE: It's true I bought it with the rest of the furniture but you've been using it as well, which means we've both contributed to its wear and tear.

HUSBAND: And the solution?

WIFE: The solution is that I alone shouldn't bear the whole cost of the old wardrobe.

HUSBAND: What shall I do now then? [*To the man*] Thanks, that's all. [*The man goes out*] Tell me what I should do now.

WIFE: Buy a second wardrobe.

HUSBAND: You mean a third.

WIFE: So I'll have a new wardrobe and you too will have a new one.

HUSBAND: It's impossible . . . and what about that one? [*Points to the old one*]

WIFE: I couldn't care less about it.

HUSBAND: [*Shouting*] It's impossible for me to buy a second wardrobe.

WIFE: You mean a third.

HUSBAND: It's impossible.

WIFE: Remember that we're solving problems, not complicating things further.

HUSBAND: But what are we going to do with this old wardrobe?

WIFE: Throw it away . . . give it to some beggar.

HUSBAND: Good God . . . some beggar . . . give a whole wardrobe to some beggar!

WIFE: After all, we wouldn't give him a section of it!

HUSBAND: Wait, I've got an idea.

WIFE: What idea? It's no good . . . I'm having the new wardrobe. Also, when I got married to you I brought along a new wardrobe; I've a right to have the new one now, especially as we are jointly responsible for the wear and tear of the old one.

HUSBAND: I'll give you the difference and we'll settle the matter.

WIFE: What difference?

HUSBAND: I'll give you five pounds for instance and you take the old one.

WIFE: [*Shouting*] Five pounds!

HUSBAND: Make it ten . . . I'll give you ten pounds.

WIFE: Impossible . . . this is a question of principle.

HUSBAND: Principle!

WIFE: Yes, principle.

HUSBAND: Listen here, listen . . . I've got an idea. You've got me muddled . . . let me tell you about the idea I've got.

WIFE: Go ahead.

HUSBAND: [*Takes a piastre from his pocket*] What's this?

WIFE: What do you mean, 'what's this?' It's a piastre piece.

HUSBAND: Good, we'll take a bet on it.

WIFE: What do you mean by a bet? I don't get you.

HUSBAND: We'll toss the piastre and agree . . . beforehand . . . if, for example, it comes out tails one of us takes the new one; if heads, the old one. The thing is to agree on something.

WIFE: So you want me to put myself at the mercy of luck.

HUSBAND: But, my dear girl, it applies to both you and me.

WIFE: All right, agreed . . . let's see what the end result is.

HUSBAND: The end result . . . [*Pause*] . . . affects both you and me. [*He holds the piastre*]

WIFE: Wait. We haven't agreed yet.

HUSBAND: Let's agree . . . make a choice. Which do you choose, heads or tails?

WIFE: Heads.

HUSBAND: And I'm tails. Fine.

WIFE: But how will you do it?

HUSBAND: Look here, I'll toss the piastre. If heads come up for you, you take the wardrobe.

WIFE: Which wardrobe?

HUSBAND: The new one, of course.

WIFE: H'm, you must be exact about things.

HUSBAND: If tails come up, I take the new wardrobe. All right? Ready? Are we agreed? I'll toss the piastre then.

WIFE: No, wait.

HUSBAND: What else is there?

WIFE: Why should *you* toss the piastre?

HUSBAND: Who should toss it then?

WIFE: Why shouldn't I?

HUSBAND: Right, and why shouldn't I?

WIFE: And why not I?

HUSBAND: And why not I?

WIFE: And why not I?

HUSBAND: And where do we go from here?

WIFE: Why should you be tossing it?

HUSBAND: Wasn't it I who made the suggestion?

WIFE: That doesn't give you the right to toss it.

HUSBAND: What will happen if I do so? You'll see the piastre turning in the air and then it will land on the floor and will continue running along till it comes to a stop.

WIFE: Even so, the way you throw it affects the result.

HUSBAND: And the solution?

WIFE: [*With indifference*] Why shouldn't I throw it? I'd throw it exactly as you would.

HUSBAND: [*As though thinking of something else*] Exactly?

WIFE: Absolutely exactly.

HUSBAND: The fact is that in order to have real fairness neither you nor I should toss it.

WIFE: Who should?

HUSBAND: We'll find someone else to toss it.

WIFE: Like who?

HUSBAND: Anybody. [*Pointing to the audience*] There in front of us are people in the street.

WIFE: [*Interrupting*] It's not reasonable for us to call someone in from the street . . . people would think we were mad.

HUSBAND: We'd explain to them the whole story from the beginning.

WIFE: Nobody'd believe it.

HUSBAND: It's not important they should believe it.

WIFE: I tell you what . . . let's both throw it together.

HUSBAND: Why shouldn't we invite someone by telephone to throw it?

WIFE: And how do I know you're not in league with him?

HUSBAND: [*Shouting*] In league with him? That's no way to talk. How could I be in league with him?

WIFE: Please don't raise your voice. Remember that we are doing all this in order that we shan't quarrel, in order that we shan't raise our voices.

HUSBAND: Really, this isn't any sort of a life.

WIFE: We must toss the piastre ourselves and face up to the situation.

HUSBAND: [*Irritably*] Explain to me how.

WIFE: Show me the piastre.

HUSBAND: [*He gives her the piastre*] Here it is.

WIFE: [*Taking the piastre from him and holding it by the rim*] Do you mind coming nearer. [*He moves closer to her*] Stretch out your hand and hold the piastre with me.

HUSBAND: [*Resignedly*] There you are, I've got hold of it.

WIFE: Now we'll raise our hands together and throw the piastre upwards . . .

HUSBAND: Don't be in such a hurry . . . wait. We must count. We can't just throw it like that, all at once.

WIFE: Who'll count?

HUSBAND: Also you and I. I'll say one and you'll say two and the moment I say three we throw it upwards.

WIFE: No, I say one and you say two and I'll be the one to say three. It's not right at all for one of us to dominate the other, there must be absolute equality.

HUSBAND: Then the solution is that I say one and you say two and then and

there we throw the piastre. Or, alternatively, you say one and I say two
and then at once we throw it.

WIFE: I'm in agreement with the first idea.

HUSBAND: Being that I should say one and you two?

WIFE: Yes.

HUSBAND: Good. That's it then. I've got no objection. But we must also
agree as to what height the piastre must go.

WIFE: To at least two metres.

HUSBAND: Yes, so that it can turn about in the air sufficiently.

WIFE: That's reasonable.

HUSBAND: And the moment it falls to the floor no one must bring it to a
stop. We'll leave it till it stops of its own accord.

WIFE: Of course.

HUSBAND: That's it then. Off we go.

WIFE: You remember that I'm heads and heads takes the new one.

HUSBAND: I do.

WIFE: Off we go.

HUSBAND: Off we go.

WIFE: Begin counting.

HUSBAND: One.

WIFE: Two.

*Immediately they hurl the piastre upwards. The piastre falls and rolls
along the floor. The two of them run after it and look.*

WIFE: [*Shouting with joy*] Heads . . . heads . . . the wardrobe's mine. [*She
runs up to the wardrobe and embraces it*] Heads . . . wardrobe.
[*Suddenly she realises that her husband is silent, so she goes to him and
gives him a loud kiss, then another, then a third*] That's it . . . smile. And
here's yet another kiss. [*She kisses him a moment later*] You said that
would be fair, didn't you? Didn't you?

HUSBAND: [*Dejectedly*] Yes.

WIFE: Then what are you annoyed about? Annoyed because you lost? After
all, someone's got to win and someone's got to lose. We must take the
matter sportingly.

HUSBAND: Sportingly?

WIFE: That's to say, like sportsmen.

HUSBAND: All right, that's fine.

WIFE: You mean you're not angry?

HUSBAND: Not at all.

WIFE: Then you'll help me move the wardrobe.

HUSBAND: I'll help you and you also help me in moving my wardrobe.

WIFE: Fine, let's start. We'll move my . . . [*Correcting herself*] . . . your wardrobe first. [*They walk up to the old wardrobe and carry it together to the left-hand side of the stage*] Where are you going to put it?

HUSBAND: What do you think about here? [*He points to a place exactly opposite the place in which it had previously stood*]

WIFE: That'll do. [*They put it down*] And then I'll put my wardrobe where it used to be . . . thus the two wardrobes will be facing each other.

HUSBAND: Come along. [*He helps her to place her wardrobe where the first one had been, then he seats himself in the armchair while she also sits down in her armchair*] There's nothing like a good rest after exerting oneself. We'll certainly both be able to sit back comfortably from now on.

WIFE: Having solved all the obstacles that lay before us.

HUSBAND: We've certainly solved most of them.

WIFE: But we must solve them all; seeing as how we've begun . . . [*Pause*] . . . we must go to the end.

HUSBAND: What's left for us to do?

WIFE: You know what's left.

HUSBAND: [*Looking around him in the room*] The television . . . the table . . . the wardrobe . . . the mirror . . . the chair I'm sitting in . . . [*Pause*] . . . it's as though they were two rooms. [*Thinking*] What's left? Ah, the record-player.

WIFE: Exactly.

HUSBAND: When I'm going to sleep I like to listen to some quiet music . . . quartets or sonatas . . . and sometimes to symphonies like Beethoven's Sixth.

WIFE: And when I'm going to sleep I like to listen to some light music, nothing complicated, nothing requiring any intellectual effort . . . I like listening to tangos.

HUSBAND: You mean we should divide up the records?

WIFE: Not only that.

HUSBAND: What should we divide then?

WIFE: What's the point of dividing up the branch of the tree if the trunk itself remains undivided.

HUSBAND: Ah, you mean the record-player itself?

WIFE: Exactly.

HUSBAND: [*Coming to a decision*] We must get ourselves a second record-player. [*Gets up and goes to the telephone*]

WIFE: And I'll be having it.

HUSBAND: It's out of the question that I give up my old record-player . . . it's been with me from my bachelor days. On it I've heard music, come to know it and understand it. It's out of the question that I ever give it up. (*Into the telephone*) Hullo.

WIFE: That's it . . . the whole thing'll be solved.

HUSBAND: [*Into the telephone*] A record-player . . . the latest model. [*Replaces the receiver. There is a knock at the door. He goes out and returns a moment later with the new record-player*] Here you are, milady.

WIFE: [*Joyfully*] I must listen to it now. [*She takes out the record of a tango and puts it on the record-player. We hear the tango. Moments pass*] Let's dance.

HUSBAND: You know I don't like dancing.

The wife dances a tango on her own.

WIFE: [*Dancing*] Heavens, if only we knew how to dance together! [*Still dancing*]

HUSBAND: Heavens, if you could only appreciate quartets and sonatas!

He hurries off to get out a Beethoven quartet and places it on his own record-player. We hear the quartet. The notes of the tango mingle with those of the quartet. Moments pass.

BOTH: [*Irritably*] It's crazy!

Each moves towards the other's record-player. He takes off the tango record, she the quartet.

HUSBAND: It's absolutely crazy.

WIFE: I was enjoying the dance.

HUSBAND: I was enjoying the quartet.

WIFE: We must find a solution.

HUSBAND: Certainly, we must find a solution . . . a solution that will allow me to listen to my quartet.

WIFE: [*Quickly*] And will allow me to listen to my tango.

HUSBAND: [*Thinking*] We must make a partition.

WIFE: A partition that we can put up when we want to listen; that will separate off that record-player from this one.

HUSBAND: And where shall we put the partition?

WIFE: Let's think about it.

HUSBAND: It doesn't need any thinking about.

WIFE: What do you mean?

HUSBAND: The partition must be half-way across the room.

WIFE: Certainly, it must be exactly half-way. How, though?

BOTH: [*Together, very quickly and as though they've discovered something*] Ah!

They kiss each other because of this discovery; then they go out, both extremely happy, and return together. The husband is carrying a large saw.

WIFE: I'll work at it from here. [*Indicating that she will sit on top of the bed*]

HUSBAND: And I'll work at it from here. [*Indicating that he will stand behind the bed. He makes his way behind the bed and stands there*] Here's exactly half-way. [*Pause*] Now you take hold of it from in front of me. [*She advances along the bed and takes hold of the saw*]

WIFE: Off we go![*They both begin sawing. Moments pass. He lets go of the saw, rolls up his sleeves and undoes his front shirt buttons. She blows on her hands and rubs them together*] Off we go! [*They start off sawing again*]

WIFE: [*As she saws*] This is a tiring business.

HUSBAND: [*As he saws*] It's tiring just now, but afterwards we'll be in clover.

WIFE: You really think so. [*Suddenly*] No, I must rest a bit. [*She lets go of the saw; he too*]

HUSBAND: Shall we have a Coca-Cola? Have you got any?

WIFE: Of course. [*She hurries out and brings back two bottles of Coca-Cola. She goes back to her place on the bed from where she offers her husband one of the bottles and keeps one for herself*] Cheers!

HUSBAND: [*Laughing*] Cheers! [*They drink*]

BOTH: [*After taking a long gulp*] Ah, that's better.

HUSBAND: To work.

WIFE: To work. [*They go back to sawing*] Like to hear some music?

HUSBAND: Don't worry . . . soon each of us will be listening to his own music in peace and quiet.

WIFE: That's so. [*The sawing continues till they have divided the bed into two halves, which are then separated from each other*]

HUSBAND: That's perfect, absolutely perfect.

WIFE: Now there's nothing left but to get a partition.

HUSBAND: I'll get the partition right away. [*He leaves the room and after a few moments we see a wooden partition appearing through the doorway. He speaks from outside*] Come and help me. [*She moves towards him and takes hold of the partition*]

WIFE: Yes . . . what do you want me to do?

HUSBAND: Pull it from your end.

WIFE: [*Pulling*] Like this?

HUSBAND: That's it.

The wooden partition comes out on to the stage, followed by the husband who is holding it by the other end. The partition is so large that when placed between the beds the stage forms two completely separate rooms.

HUSBAND: Careful . . . keep hold of it. [*The husband is now in the right-hand room and the wife in the left-hand one*]. Yes . . . ex . . . actly.

BOTH: Heavens . . . a room of my own!

They go out and each changes round . . . the husband is now in the left-hand room and the wife in the right-hand one.

HUSBAND: [*Raising his voice*] What do you think? Can you hear me?

WIFE: [*Raising her voice*] Do you think any sound can filter through to you? Tell me . . . can you hear me?

HUSBAND: Why don't you answer?

WIFE: Why don't you answer?

A moment later they both move away from the partition. He puts the quartet on the record-player. At the same time she puts the tango on her player. He sits down in the armchair, while she dances a tango, moving round the room. He quietly leaves the chair and stretches out on the bed. It is clear that he is greatly enjoying the music. She is still dancing the tango. This situation continues for some time.

CURTAIN

The Wheat Well

Ali Salem

The Wheat Well *by Ali Salem*

Cast

BASSIOUNI	EMPLOYEE ONE
MITWALLI	EMPLOYEE TWO
UNCLE HUSSEIN	EMPLOYEE THREE
DR WAHID	EMPLOYEE FOUR
DR WAHID-HYPHEN	EMPLOYEE FIVE
	EMPLOYEE SIX
	OTHER EMPLOYEES

Place: *A vast desert*
Time: *A few moments after sunset*

Set: *A wooden contraption resembling an oil rig though very small, no more than the height of a man.* MITWALLI *is fixing the rivets of the rig with an iron lever and from time to time hammering in a nail. Near him lies* UNCLE HUSSEIN *who is examining a large strip of paper in the light from a kerosene lamp of the type used in mines. Near them lies* BASSIOUNI *wrapped in a blanket; he stirs uneasily under the blanket in a way that gives the impression he is unable to get to sleep.*

BASSIOUNI: The blanket's full of sand. [*He looks at his watch*] Good heavens, it's stopped. It seems it's also full of sand. What's the time now, Uncle Hussein?
HUSSEIN: [*Preoccupied*] 7.30.

BASSIOUNI *covers himself up with the blanket and lies down again.*

MITWALLI: Still two rivets to do, Uncle Hussein.

MITWALLI *hammers away.*

BASSIOUNI: [*Starting up in alarm*] What are you up to, brother? Have some consideration . . . can't you see you've got someone sleeping beside you?

What's all this banging that's going on? [*Once again he covers himself up angrily*]

MITWALLI: It's finished, Bassiouni . . . just one more rivet. [*He hammers softly*]

BASSIOUNI: [*Waking up again*] Man . . . man . . . I'm telling you, I want to go to sleep. Look here, you've made it so I can't sleep any longer.

MITWALLI *looks at him in silence and goes back to his work. He appears to wish to avoid getting into a squabble with him.*

BASSIOUNI: [*Chewing something, then spitting it out noisily*] Lousy sand. Even the food's full of sand. Everything's got sand in it. For seven years I've been up to my ears in sand with you in the desert. Seven years in the freezing cold and the blistering heat.

MITWALLI: [*Calming him down*] Take it easy Bassiouni.

BASSIOUNI: Don't worry about me, young fellow. I don't want your advice. You save your words for yourself. [*Mitwalli mumbles*] Eh? What are you saying? What are you mumbling about? I'm not to your liking, is that it? God curse the days that brought us together, brother.

HUSSEIN: Hey, Bassiouni, what is it? What's wrong?

BASSIOUNI: Nothing's wrong. I'm bored, fed up, had it.

MITWALLI: [*Trying to calm him down*] Bassiouni, I didn't say . . .

BASSIOUNI: [*Jumping up and shouting as he throws the blanket aside*] Don't say 'Bassiouni' . . . understand? Don't say Bassiouni. D'you think you're my friend or something? Don't say Bassiouni . . . understand?

MITWALLI: [*Keeping calm*] I'm sorry, Bassiouni. What do you want me to call you?

BASSIOUNI: [*In a rage*] I'm telling you not to say . . .

MITWALLI: [*Shouting, he too having lost his temper*] God Almighty! Why don't you tell me what to call you, and I'll call you it? God Almighty! What's he all het up about? Shall I call you Bassiouni Bey?

BASSIOUNI: So you want to mock me, do you, want to make fun of me? You don't know what to call me? You tell him, Uncle Hussein.

MITWALLI: Right . . . fine . . . I understand. You could have let me know, though, without all this fuss. As you wish, Mr Bassiouni . . . though for seven years you've been just Bassiouni.

BASSIOUNI: That was seven years ago, but now I'm not going to give up any of my rights. Understand? Yes, I'm an educated person and I'm well aware of my rights. Now I want to know, what are we doing?

MITWALLI: We're digging in the desert.

BASSIOUNI: I'm not talking to you, man. I'm talking to Uncle Hussein.

HUSSEIN: [*Quietly*] You talking to me, Bassiouni?

BASSIOUNI: Who d'you think I'm talking to? . . . my father?

HUSSEIN: What do you want to know exactly?

BASSIOUNI: We've been digging away in the desert for seven years . . . what are we looking for?

HUSSEIN: And why have you kept quiet for seven years?

BASSIOUNI: I'm a free agent.

HUSSEIN: Not at all, you're not free or anything like it. This has got nothing to do with being free. It's your circumstances that have improved and so you've begun to ask questions and quarrel.

BASSIOUNI: Improved or not, it's no one else's business. What are we looking for?

HUSSEIN: You'll know later.

BASSIOUNI: When later?

HUSSEIN: When we find it.

BASSIOUNI: Find what?

HUSSEIN: What we're looking for.

BASSIOUNI: [*Exploding*] What is it? Oil? They don't search for oil like this. Diamonds? There are no diamonds in the desert. Gold? Iron?

HUSSEIN: This part of the desert has got none of these things . . . and if there were, this drill wouldn't be any good for them anyway.

BASSIOUNI: Then what are we looking for?

HUSSEIN: You should respect the contract that's between you and me. One of the conditions of the contract is that you mustn't ask what we're looking for. You're just working with me and that's that. Why is it that Mitwalli is working and not saying anything?

BASSIOUNI: 'Cos he's stupid, 'cos he's ignorant.

MITWALLI: [*With extreme calm and politeness*] Mr Bassiouni, Mr Bassiouni . . . d'you see how I'm calling you Mr Bassiouni? Mr Bassiouni, you're being rude.

BASSIOUNI: That's just great. See? How do you like that? I end up being made fun of in front of you. Does the contract also say I should be made fun of?

HUSSEIN: You want to insult him and for him not to answer back? Listen, Bassiouni, calm down, son. Calm down and be sensible. I know your nerves are in a bad way these days . . . it's sitting around in the desert that makes one like that.

BASSIOUNI: [*Hysterically*] No, I'm very calm and very sensible. The desert's done nothing to me. I could stay a hundred years in the desert and I'd be quite calm and my nerves would be fine.

HUSSEIN: Fine. You work and you eat and you drink and you take your wages. I haven't exploited you in any way.

BASSIOUNI: You haven't exploited me in any way? All this and you haven't exploited me? And the seven years of my life I've wasted in the desert?

HUSSEIN: You haven't wasted them. When you first came to work with me you could scarcely read or write. It's I who've taught you and made you take the secondary school certificate and the university entrance exam; it's I who've put you down for the university. It was you who used to come to me, Bassiouni, and now you're Mr Bassiouni, prospective student at the Faculty of Commerce. The seven years haven't gone for nothing.

BASSIOUNI: Even so I'm only human, brother. Just because you've helped me, do you have to make a slave of me? What d'you think I am? A water buffalo going round in a water-wheel without knowing why it's going round? I don't care what's written in the contract . . . I now want to know what we're looking for. I want to know what's written on the paper you're reading and which you keep in the belt round your waist.

HUSSEIN: You wouldn't be able to read it.

BASSIOUNI: You tell me what's written on it.

MITWALLI: That's it, Uncle Hussein. The rig's set up. Everything's ready for drilling.

UNCLE HUSSEIN *rises to his feet and folds up the piece of paper and places it carefully in his belt.*

HUSSEIN: Keep these questions for the morning, Bassiouni. I'll answer you later. Now let's get down to work. Give me a hand.

BASSIOUNI: No, I'm not getting up. I'm not putting a hand to anything until I know what we're doing.

HUSSEIN: Be sensible, Bassiouni. Get up and work and tomorrow early you can leave us.

BASSIOUNI: Leave you, leave you and return to Cairo to tell them what? What shall I tell my relatives I've been working at? Don't tell me it's buried treasure you've been searching around for, and you've got the map showing where it is. These sorts of things only happen in films.

MITWALLI: Once, I swear, someone found some treasure where we live in Sayyida.

BASSIOUNI: In Sayyida maybe, but not in the desert. [*A moment of silence*] I don't want to know what we're doing. I'll ask another question: Who are you? What are you?

HUSSEIN: An Egyptologist.

BASSIOUNI: Liar . . . you're a waiter. Here's your identity card. [*He takes the card from his pocket*] A waiter at the Ammon Café. D'you hear, friend Mitwalli, this Uncle Hussein of yours has made a fool of us. He's not an Egyptologist or anything of the sort.

MITWALLI: Waiter, Egyptologist, it doesn't matter. What matters to me is that he's Uncle Hussein and that's all.

BASSIOUNI: Then why is he lying? A waiter in Egyptologist's clothing? Take care he's not a spy.

HUSSEIN: Your nerves are really in a bad way, Bassiouni.

BASSIOUNI: [*His attitude changing to one of open entreaty*] By the Prophet, Uncle Hussein, by the Prophet, may God keep you safe, master. I'll kiss your feet . . . [*He breaks down weeping*] . . . if you'll just tell me what we're looking for.

HUSSEIN: Calm down, son. Calm down, Bassiouni.

BASSIOUNI: [*Bursting out crying like a small child*] I'm like your son, Uncle Hussein. God keep you safe, Master. God keep you safe.

HUSSEIN: [*Calming him down*] Fine. Fine. That's enough, I'll tell everything. Our search was going to end tonight. I was intending to tell you tomorrow morning. Whether I'd found what we were looking for or not, I was going to tell you. Leave the rig, Mitwalli. Come and sit here next to Bassiouni. I'll explain everything. It's true I'm a waiter, but I've got a good knowledge of Egyptology. [*Silence*] I'm looking for wheat.

BASSIOUNI: What?

HUSSEIN: Wheat . . . a wheat well.

BASSIOUNI: Wheat? Are there such things as wheat wells?

HUSSEIN: Yes, there are.

BASSIOUNI: It's not just you who are mad . . . you're mad and I'm crazy for going along with you. D'you hear, Mr Mitwalli? He's looking for wheat . . . wheat under the desert. No one's going to find any wheat, Uncle Hussein. Wheat is grown. [*He seeks* MITWALLI's *support*] Mitwalli, you are a peasant by origin . . . it is grown, isn't it?

MITWALLI: I'll believe anything Uncle Hussein says.

BASSIOUNI: Of course. Because you're stupid . . . though there's no one as stupid and mad as him. For seven years we've been looking for something that doesn't exist. If only you'd told us to begin with we'd have let you know that wheat was something that was grown.

HUSSEIN: Everybody in the world knows that wheat is grown.

BASSIOUNI: You want to tell us there are fields sown with wheat under the ground?

HUSSEIN: No, the wheat hasn't been sown under ground, it's stored underground.

BASSIOUNI: And who's stored it? The Germans or the Allies?

HUSSEIN: They themselves hadn't enough to eat. Those people left nothing in the desert but mines and corpses.

BASSIOUNI: Then who stored the wheat?

HUSSEIN: The ancient Egyptians.

BASSIOUNI: What are you saying?

HUSSEIN: The ancient Egyptians. They stored enormous quantities of wheat in the desert.

BASSIOUNI: My mind's going. I'll go mad. If you were to tell me that you're looking for a graveyard full of gold I might well believe you. What do you know about Egyptology? What's turned you from a waiter into an Egyptologist?

HUSSEIN: Will you let me finish what I was going to say or shall I let you go on torturing yourself?

MITWALLI: Man, let the man speak. Go on, speak, Uncle Hussein. I'm with you.

BASSIOUNI: Be so good as to tell me what made me waste seven years . . less a quarter of an hour.

HUSSEIN: Like it's written in the identity card you found, or which maybe you stole, I'm a waiter at the Ammon Café which is alongside the Egyptian Museum. I stayed in that café for twenty years. The employees working in the museum would spend their mornings in the museum and afterwards they'd come and sit at the café with their things. They'd take tea and afterwards they'd stay on working, and sometimes they'd forget the odd statue or a bit of papyrus, some old piece of something. As time went on and we'd mix with them, they'd give their orders in hieroglyphics and we'd sit together and chat.

BASSIOUNI: In hieroglyphics?

HUSSEIN: Yes, I began to study the things they left in the café. I had someone working with me, God rest his soul, who was keen on Roman archaeology. He went off to look for Alexander's grave in Alexandria, while I took a whole life's savings and came to look for the wheateries.

BASSIOUNI: The wheat what?

HUSSEIN: Wheateries . . . like granaries.

MITWALLI: [*With intense admiration*] Carry on, Uncle Hussein. Carry on. Let him go on, Mr Bassiouni.

HUSSEIN: Inside any royal tomb they discover they find vessels containing a little wheat for the king to eat when he wakes up. You know of course that they believed in an afterlife.

BASSIOUNI: I know, I know.

HUSSEIN: The question that exercised me was, 'Fine, that was the wheat for the kings, but where did the ordinary people put their wheat?' I was sure that the ordinary people had been putting their wheat in places no one had yet discovered. I sat down to study the matter until by chance I came across the cover of some lecture notes of an ancient Egyptian student at the University of Thebes. The notebook had these instructions written on it. [*He takes out the large piece of paper from under his belt*]

BASSIOUNI: What are you going to read? You can invent anything.

HUSSEIN: All right, so I won't read it. You who're so educated, you read it.

BASSIOUNI: And from where would I know how to read hieroglyphics?

MITWALLI: That's that then, Mr Bassiouni . . . seeing that you don't know how to read hieroglyphics, let him read it to us. You read, Uncle Hussein.

HUSSEIN: These instructions are those of an ancient Egyptian sage who says: [*He reads*] 'O my son . . . Cleanliness is part of faith . . . O my son, when the flood waters cover the earth and you find no land to cultivate, go with your comrades to build the Pyramids. After thousands of years people will come to look at this great building and will pay much money with which you will improve your conditions.'

BASSIOUNI: Is that so? He didn't say they'd pay in hard currency?

HUSSEIN: Making fun of me are you? That's what is written . . . I'm not making anything up.

BASSIOUNI: No. Carry on.

HUSSEIN: The important bit of advice is the bit that's coming; 'O my son, when you harvest the wheat, take a large quantity of it and place it in the city wheatery, for this wheat will be of use to you when you are resurrected anew.' For twenty years I'd been studying until I found out that every village had its own wheatery, that's to say what we call a silo, in the shape of an enormous clay jar buried in the desert. Each person would go every Friday, also on feast days, to put a little wheat into it, and they stored it up for the Day of Resurrection.

MITWALLI: That's reasonable, Uncle Hussein, very reasonable. Do you get it, Mr Bassiouni? . . . so that when one wakes up from being dead one will find something to eat, or else one would die of hunger all over again.

HUSSEIN: Just imagine it, thousands of people over thousands of years, storing wheat. You can just imagine the quantity of wheat that's been stored away.

BASSIOUNI: Prove what you've said.

MITWALLI: I believe you, Uncle Hussein.

BASSIOUNI: Well, suppose we find this wheatery of yours, how long will it last us for? A day? It won't last us a single meal.

MITWALLI: God willing, brother, everyone will have himself a mouthful . . . it will still be something to keep one going.

HUSSEIN: No, I've calculated the size and I've calculated our daily consumption. One wheatery will be sufficient for us for fifty years at least. For the last seven years we've been finding the walls of the wheatery. But tonight we're going to discover its opening. Its opening is one metre from the earth's surface. As for the bottom, it's at a distance of three thousand metres.

MITWALLI: Goodness, and this wheat's all right for eating, Uncle Hussein?

HUSSEIN: Of course, it's top grade, the sort you make cakes of, the best quality wheat.

BASSIOUNI: All right for eating, you idiot? Do you think I believe one word of what's been said?

HUSSEIN: [Resolutely] You're free to believe or not. My calculations are exact and according to my study the opening of the wheatery is here.

BASSIOUNI: Meaning that if we drill here, wheat will come out?

HUSSEIN: God willing.

BASSIOUNI: [Sarcastically] And how will it come out? In a fountain? In a fountain and then we'll pass it through pipes and pack it into sacks?

HUSSEIN: Your trouble is that you don't dream, that you're deprived of imagination, and so it's impossible for you ever to believe in anything. I'm very sorry that I taught you. You're going to be a very dangerous educated person.

BASSIOUNI: What do you mean, dream? I'm an intelligent person and I'm still convinced that wheat is grown. Anyway, as the proverb says, 'Water tests the diver' . . . let's start drilling.

They gather round the rig and work on lowering the pipe.

HUSSEIN: [*Pleadingly*] O Lord, don't dash my hopes.

BASSIOUNI: Forty centimetres . . .

HUSSEIN: O Lord, this wheat is wanted by people . . . by people, O Almighty God.

MITWALLI: O Lord, don't dash Uncle Hussein's hopes.

HUSSEIN: O Lord, just so Bassiouni won't gloat over us.

BASSIOUNI: A metre, and there's nothing.

HUSSEIN: Go deeper.

BASSIOUNI: Didn't you say it was a metre down?

HUSSEIN: [*Angrily*] Go down deeper.

BASSIOUNI: One metre and twenty centimetres.

HUSSEIN: O Lord, I've studied it carefully and my calculations are correct. O Lord, I'm a decent chap and I've never done anything to make You angry. I've never even taken tips from anyone my whole life, nor have I short-changed anybody. O Lord, just to oblige me. [*A moment's silence*] Take out the drill.

BASSIOUNI *takes out the drill and* UNCLE HUSSEIN *collects it up and bangs it against the stage floor. A small quantity of wheat falls from it.*

HUSSEIN: [*Crazy with elation*] Wheat . . . wheat . . . lots and lots of wheat. It'll last us for fifty years at least. I've discovered the wheat. I've made history.

BASSIOUNI: [*Challenging him*] So it's you who've discovered it? And what about me? Was I just playing around? Eh? Just playing around, was I? Your Honour wants to enter history all on your own! That's right, show yourself in your true colours!

HUSSEIN: In my true colours?

BASSIOUNI: You're selfish. You think only of yourself. All you want is to enter history on your own.

HUSSEIN: And you want to enter? Come along then, enter. Anyone stopping you?

BASSIOUNI: So this is how all my work for you ends! You make fun of me, you insult me. Now you're the big man, the great man? And a short while ago you were standing in front of the good Lord like a kitten. Do you see, Mitwalli? He was wanting to give us the impression he was an Egyptologist and wanted to feed people. Now he's been exposed. All he wants is to enter history.

MITWALLI: Let him enter. God grant him good health. Uncle Hussein deserves the very best. Go ahead and enter history, Uncle Hussein.

During this time MITWALLI *has been collecting up his tools.*

BASSIOUNI: I'm telling you, he wants to steal our hard work, he wants to steal our sweat.

HUSSEIN: You're an ignorant good-for-nothing. I really regret all the trouble I've taken over you. What do you think history is, my boy? A cinema that someone with a ticket can just go in to? You think anyone enters history just because he fancies it? It's history that chooses. [*He turns to* MITWALLI] We've found the wheat, Mitwalli. Rejoice, Mitwalli. [*He notices that* MITWALLI *is downcast*] Mitwalli, are you collecting up the equipment?

BASSIOUNI: He's collecting up his own belongings as well.

HUSSEIN: What's wrong, Mitwalli? Has something upset you.

MITWALLI: [*Continuing to gather up his belongings*] Not at all.

HUSSEIN: Good God, what's wrong, Mitwalli? There are tears in your eyes. You're crying Mitwalli, instead of rejoicing. We've found what we were looking for, Mitwalli. We've found the wheat.

BASSIOUNI: All that and you don't want him to be annoyed, you don't want him to cry and lament bitterly too? After we've wasted our lives with you in the desert, you want to exploit the sweat of our brows. You want to steal all the fame and all the glory for yourself.

HUSSEIN: Don't believe it, Mitwalli. The fellow's misleading you. I'm not like that at all. When the papers take pictures, they'll take pictures of the three of us. On the radio the three of us will talk. On the television and the cinema the three of us will appear together. I swear to you by my honour. All the fame and all the glory will be for the three of us.

MITWALLI: What fame, what glory are you talking about, Uncle Hussein? I'm not one for these things in any case. Half a kilogram of kebab, five Belmont cigarettes and a glass of tea is more worthwhile than all the glory in the world. These things are understood by Mr Bassiouni, because he's Mr Bassiouni and I'm just Mitwalli. You made one mistake, Uncle Hussein. [UNCLE HUSSEIN *looks at him questioningly*] When you came to teach Bassiouni you should have taught him to understand me.

BASSIOUNI: I understand you well, Mitwalli.

MITWALLI: You would have had respect for me. What a pity you don't understand me and the likes of you don't understand the likes of me. For seven years you've been working with me on one rig and you've put up a wall between us. For seven years you've been working and talking with your nose in the air. Even if you once forgot and said 'Good morning', you'd say it with your nose in the air. I didn't care about the cold, I didn't care about the heat. All the sand of the desert was one heap, but the sand that was in your behaviour made a second one. [*Bitterly*] Mr Bassiouni, do you think I too haven't got something to put on airs about? I was something really big back home. I was Mitwalli, Mitwalli with the golden foot.

BASSIOUNI: Golden what?

MITWALLI: Yes, everyone who saw me when I played football said that I had a great future. I used to play really beautifully, Uncle Hussein.

BASSIOUNI: Rubbish. If you'd been a great player they'd have taken you into one of the big clubs and we'd have heard of your name long ago.

MITWALLI: I did actually go. Someone took me to a really big club. They kept me hanging about for twelve hours till the man responsible came to see me play. I swear, Uncle Hussein, it was twelve hours. When the man responsible came to see me . . . [*His voice chokes*] . . . I wasn't able to play . . . I couldn't run . . .

HUSSEIN: Why not? Were you scared?

MITWALLI: I'm never scared. [*Dejected and shamefaced*] I hadn't had any breakfast. [*Distressed*] If only they'd told me that they'd keep me hanging about so long before I played, I'd have somehow managed to have something for breakfast. By now my name would have spread far and wide and Bassiouni would long ago have been calling me 'Captain'.

BASSIOUNI: Have you been holding out on me?

MITWALLI: Holding out on you about what? I'm not up to you. Don't be silly, man, I wouldn't do that.

BASSIOUNI: I'm sorry, Mitwalli, if I've upset you. The past is over and done with. We're living in today. Listen, Mitwalli, we must stand together. We must make a pact. We must form one front, otherwise we'll get swallowed up.

HUSSEIN: You really are pathetic . . . who, son, would be swallowing you up?

BASSIOUNI: You of course.

HUSSEIN: God bless us and keep us!

BASSIOUNI: Then why do you think that Mitwalli's so sad and is crying?

He's been upset by you, but he's shy with you and doesn't want to be
rude, so he takes it out on me. And I accept it from him because he's my
mate and we've shared meals together. Don't be afraid, Mitwalli.
[*Ingratiating himself with him*] I'll get you all your rights.

MITWALLI: [*Pushing him away*] Man, get away from me. Let me be. That's
all lies, Uncle Hussein. I'm sad because of something else. [*A moment
of silence*] I'm sad because the work's finished. That's it, we've found
the wheat, and as of tomorrow I'll once again be unemployed. All my
life I've been working five days and out of work ten. With you, Uncle
Hussein, I've worked for seven years. For seven years and I've not had a
worry. I was frightened about the day when we'd find what we were
looking for. Uncle Hussein, a man who's without work isn't worth
anything, he's a nothing.

HUSSEIN: Don't be silly, who said the work's finished? The work hasn't
started yet. From tomorrow hundreds of lorries will arrive to carry off
the wheat and take it to all the houses, all the villages. Our real project
starts tomorrow. Do you think our job is just to find the wheat? Our real
job is to find it and to deliver it to every stomach. Don't worry, Mitwalli,
we'll be working for fifty years. We'll save money and people will come
and take over from us. You've got to realise something . . . this desert
hasn't got just this one wheatery; the desert's full of wheateries.

MITWALLI: Is that so, Uncle Hussein?

HUSSEIN: For sure. Don't worry. There'll be no unemployment from now
on. There's work, there's work to be done. You'll go on working and
making money and saving. From now on you won't be a nothing ever
again. We three will be working till we die.

BASSIOUNI: Are we going to stay on here all the time?

HUSSEIN: Of course.

BASSIOUNI: So I'll not be able to attend my courses at the college?

HUSSEIN: We'll get around to thinking about that later. As for now
we've got to send some cables to Cairo. I've still got a hundred pounds
on me. I'll send cables for the whole amount.

MITWALLI: Now?

HUSSEIN: Yes, now.

MITWALLI: In the morning's better, Uncle Hussein. In daytime you can see
your way. There's thirty kilometres of desert between us and the nearest
cable post, and the desert's full of wolves.

HUSSEIN: I can't wait till morning. The cables have got to go out now to the
people responsible, to their homes and offices, also to the newspapers,

the radio and the television. All the media must direct their attention here tomorrow.

BASSIOUNI: Is that the sort of trick to play on me, Uncle Hussein? If only you'd let me know from the beginning, I'd have had a clean, well-ironed shirt ready. Like this my photo'll come out in the papers with me looking like a convict.

UNCLE HUSSEIN *looks at him in astonishment, then turns his face away.*

HUSSEIN: I'll run. Don't worry yourselves about me. I'll go and come straight back. [UNCLE HUSSEIN *runs on the spot, far away from the other two. He runs with swift, active steps*]

MITWALLI: [*Calling out, cupping his hands round his mouth*] Mind the wolves, Uncle Hussein. Be careful.

HUSSEIN: [*Shouting and continuing to run*] Don't worry about me.

MITWALLI: Mr Bassiouni, it's not right to let him run off on his own in the desert. I'll go and keep him company.

BASSIOUNI: And leave me here on my own so that something can pop out and eat me?

MITWALLI: Light a little wood and nothing will come anywhere near you.

BASSIOUNI: No, man, you make a fire and I'll go with him.

MITWALLI: You won't be able to run all that way.

BASSIOUNI: Do you think no one but you knows how to run?

BASSIOUNI *runs off and catches up with* UNCLE HUSSEIN. *They run along-together.*

HUSSEIN: Hey, Bassiouni? Have you left Mitwalli on his own?

BASSIOUNI: Don't worry about him. I explained to him that he should make a bit of a fire. If he makes a fire there's nothing will come anywhere near him. You see, he was frightened something would pop out and eat him.

A period of silence during which they both continue running.

BASSIOUNI: There was something I wanted to say.

HUSSEIN: What?

BASSIOUNI: Are you going to write Mitwalli's name with mine?

HUSSEIN: Of course. Why not?

BASSIOUNI: You see, he doesn't know English, and you know of course that we'll be sitting at conferences and there'll be foreigners there. Suppose someone asks him: [*Speaking in English*] 'What's your name?'

HUSSEIN: You're quite right . . . Mitwalli doesn't know English, but he did know how to carry the rig around for seven years. In any case, if someone asked him: [*Speaking in English*] 'What is your name?' Your Honour could always translate for him.

BASSIOUNI *is exhausted and slows down.*

BASSIOUNI: Take it easy, Uncle Hussein.

UNCLE HUSSEIN *slows down.*

BASSIOUNI: Slow down a lot, Uncle Hussein.

HUSSEIN: That's just what I'm doing.

BASSIOUNI: I can't run.

HUSSEIN: All right, then . . . go back.

BASSIOUNI: [*In terror*] Go back on my own?

HUSSEIN: What do you want me to do for you?

BASSIOUNI: Carry me.

HUSSEIN: Carry you?

BASSIOUNI: Please, Uncle Hussein, by the Prophet. Didn't you used to carry me?

HUSSEIN: Yes, I used to, but you were a lot lighter in those days.

BASSIOUNI: [*Panting and beseeching*] Carry me, Uncle Hussein. Please, I can't go on.

UNCLE HUSSEIN *stops, then puts him up on his shoulders and starts moving off with difficulty.* BASSIOUNI *comfortably seated, takes out a cigarette, lights it and takes a long draw at it.*

BASSIOUNI: Do you know, Uncle Hussein . . . ?

HUSSEIN: [*Mumbling*] H'm.

BASSIOUNI: Do you know that night-time in the desert has got a very mysterious magic. [*Overwhelmed*] How marvellous!

HUSSEIN: Is that so?

BASSIOUNI: One finds that even the stars in the desert, the way they glitter, is more beautiful than the way they glitter in Cairo. Do you know,

Uncle Hussein, the most important thing in the world is the feeling for beauty. My goodness! Incidentally, people in Cairo really are unfortunate. It strikes me that the most urgent problem in Cairo is that of transport. How do you think we can solve it for people?

HUSSEIN: They could ride on me.

BASSIOUNI: I'm talking seriously, Uncle Hussein. This is a really serious question, it could hinder plans for growth. In my opinion it's more serious than the problem of birth control. The thing that surprises me is how a genius like you can't feel the magic and beauty that is around us.

HUSSEIN: The fact is, son, that you're riding, and the one who rides has a better feeling for beauty than the one who carries.

They proceed off stage with BASSIOUNI *still talking.*

BASSIOUNI: Good heavens! In the city one's eye bumps up against buildings, but here one can allow the eye to enjoy itself as far as it can see. There's nothing but sand and the stars. Even the sound of the wolves completes the symphony of beauty. [*With feeling*] How marvellous!

They go out.

They return again with UNCLE HUSSEIN *still carrying* BASSIOUNI. *He puts him down near the sleeping* MITWALLI.

BASSIOUNI: [*Addressing himself to* MITWALLI] It's just as well I went with Uncle Hussein. Do you know, Mitwalli, the man at the cable place didn't have a pencil. All the cables were written with my pencil. [*He takes out his pencil and looks at it admiringly*] You see, I don't go anywhere without a pencil. Mitwalli! [*He shakes him*] Mitwalli!

HUSSEIN: [*In a tired voice*] Let him sleep. It's the first time he's had a deep sleep for seven years. Oh, my shoulder's killing me.

BASSIOUNI: What's wrong, Uncle Hussein?

HUSSEIN: My shoulder and back.

BASSIOUNI: It must be rheumatism.

HUSSEIN: Not at all. It feels like some cancer that the good Lord's afflicted me with.

BASSIOUNI: God forbid, man! Don't say such a thing. You'll find it's just a touch of rheumatism. But probably it's neither rheumatism nor anything of the sort. Could be that you got tired carrying me.

HUSSEIN: Could be. [*Yawns*] Good night, Bassiouni. [BASSIOUNI *also prepares his bedding for sleep*]

BASSIOUNI: [*Pulling the cover over himself*] The whole world's going to be upside down here tomorrow. [*As though addressing a group of people*] Be so good, please . . . let's not have any pictures . . no pictures. We're not film stars, we're anonymous heroes . . . we're just simple people . . . How did we manage to stand up to the hardships of the desert? That's a good question. I'll tell you, whenever I was tired and felt a desire to run away I would think of all the simple people who were in need of the wheat. I would think of the open mouths that were awaiting the result of our ordeal . . . Of course . . . Of course . . . Sometimes my companions would feel despair, but I would encourage them and fill them with enthusiasm . . . . You see, the point is that I've studied how to inspire men with enthusiasm . . . Please, I would ask you not to take any pictures . . . I'm a very simple person.

He slurs the words as sleep steals over him. The lighting grows dimmer until the stage is in utter darkness.

Suddenly all the lights go on at once. Over the microphones in the auditorium we hear hundreds of thousands of voices shouting wildly, ferociously: 'Za . . . ma . . . lek. Look and see what Al-Ahli's up to.'* The shouts reverberate in a frightening way so that our three heroes start from their sleep in terror. At the same time the stage is subjected to another invasion, by a mass of people, the greatest number that the stage will hold, wearing dark suits and carrying cameras, lighting equipment, broadcasting equipment and notebooks. Workmen put down powerful spotlights, then turn them on so that for some moments they shine into the eyes of the whole audience, then the lighting concentrates on a person wearing a white suit, DR WAHID. *The photographers push and jostle one another in their attempts to photograph* DR WAHID, *trying to hear what he has to say and to direct their questions at him. Our three heroes are taken aback. Vainly they try to talk with any one of the journalists.* DR WAHID *talks in an earnest and captivating manner.*

DR WAHID: This discovery is a thousand times more important than that of the sun ships. The wheat is present in quantities which we cannot at

---

*Zamalek and Al-Ahli are the names of football teams.

present know. What you must know though is that this discovery is to be regarded as a first step which will lead to a second step, the second step being the important one . . . the discovery of the wheateries.

JOURNALIST: A question, Dr Wahid: did the explorations take a long time?

DR WAHID: The explorations relating to the wheateries are explorations that have been going on for a very long time. They've been going on for about two hundred years. They were interrupted for reasons which there is no point in going into now. After that they were continued for reasons which, in the interests of secrecy, I do not now have the right to divulge.

While DR WAHID *is delivering his statement, the journalists stand in groups singing in different tones of voice: 'Za . . . ma . . . lek. Look . . . see what Al-Ahli's up to.'*

DR WAHID: The theoretical basis of all these explorations is the beliefs of the ancient Egyptians. They used to believe that there was another life, and for the purpose of this other life they would place in their tombs certain things which they could use after they were brought back to life. Among these were things to eat. [*The chorus of journalists is still active*] There is a common belief expressed in the popular legends that of the seven granaries in which Joseph stored wheat, six of them still exist under the ground. This was because they needed only a single granary to cope with the famine that occurred then.

JOURNALIST: Do you think that something other than wheat could be provided for us to eat?

DR WAHID: Yes, the public relations department has made provisions for a cup of tea and a light lunch. We're very sorry but you appreciate of course that the project is still a new one and this place is fairly isolated. We would have liked to give you a hot lunch. That is the end of the statement. Please go ahead and have your meals. [*Shouting*] Please go ahead.

They rush out at the same speed as they entered and we hear the same shouts. Silence reigns for a while. DR WAHID *approaches* UNCLE HUSSEIN *smiling.*

DR WAHID: Hullo, Uncle Hussein.
HUSSEIN: Hullo, Dr Wahid.

DR WAHID: Where have you been, man? Ever since you left the café the things they've been serving have been really lousy. How are you, Uncle Hussein?

HUSSEIN: God keep you.

DR WAHID: Excuse me, Uncle Hussein, I've got a bone to pick with you . . . and you know I've got your interests at heart . . . have you read my latest book?

HUSSEIN: I've read all the books available on Egyptology. When did Your Honour's book appear?

DR WAHID: About a year ago.

HUSSEIN: I'm sorry. Your Honour knows that I've been in the desert for seven years.

DR WAHID: There you are, if only you'd read it you wouldn't have got yourself into this fix, and me along with you.

HUSSEIN: I got you into a fix?

DR WAHID: Yes, I said in my book that there wasn't any wheat in the desert.

HUSSEIN: But I found it.

DR WAHID: That's just what's so frightful. The book's now valueless. You've turned me into an ignoramus. How can I show my face again in scholarly circles? At all events, these are mere points of view. Fine, Uncle Hussein, the best of luck to you. A very goodbye to you. We'll issue you right away with a travel voucher, first-class air-conditioned, for you and those with you.

HUSSEIN: I don't understand at all.

DR WAHID: It's the theoretical side of the question that was your concern. That's over and done with. Now we'll begin the stage that concerns us. It's we who will be carrying out the project.

HUSSEIN: [*Dumbfounded*] And me?

DR WAHID: You'll get a medal. The scholarly body you belong to will put you up for a medal.

HUSSEIN: Scholarly body I belong to? The Trade Union of Waiters? The Trade Union of Waiters will put me up for a medal for Egyptology? Please, Doctor, I don't want any medals. I don't want to leave the project.

DR WAHID: We'll discuss that matter later. [*Shouting*] Desks!

We hear the same shouts and the workmen begin hurrying on to the stage carrying a large number of desks. The desks are brought on to the stage

from all directions. MITWALLI *hugs the rig in order to protect it
from the desks; he withdraws with it from the path of the desks that rush
down upon him. The desks pursue him, and* MITWALLI *goes down from the
stage into the auditorium. The desks continue to pursue the rig in their
attempts to occupy the theatre and find a place for themselves.* MITWALLI
*retreats before them carrying the rig until he leaves by the auditorium door
into the street. With him are* UNCLE HUSSEIN *and* BASSIOUNI*. The desks now
occupy the stage and part of the auditorium.*

DR WAHID: [*Shouting*] Employees!

The same number of EMPLOYEES *as there are desks come on stage with
lightning speed and take their places. On their chests are hung numbers
reading 1, 2, 3, etc.*

DR WAHID: [*Watching the entrance of the employees as though directing
   a battle*] One . . . two . . . three . . . four . . .

After the EMPLOYEES *have taken their places, three office boys enter
carrying large quantities of papers and files. They swoop down on the
desks, distribute the papers, then immediately leave. The whole of this
scene must be played with great speed and regularity of movement.* DR
WAHID *stands facing the* EMPLOYEES.

DR WAHID: Please pay attention. I have been entrusted with administering
   this project and I must make a success of it. I have a personal dislike of
   failure, and therefore anyone deliberately at fault or guilty of neglect or
   acting in an irresponsible manner will be shown no mercy by me. We've
   got a job of work to do here. Understood? Bureaucratic employees who
   obstruct everything and complicate everything, those lazy people we
   always see portrayed on stage, radio and television, I'll not allow their
   presence here. Understood? I'm warning you as of now . . . where work
   is concerned I'd not show favour to my own father. I'll not tolerate any
   laziness. And yet with all that I'm very democratic. I won't tell you that
   the door of my office is open. No, I haven't got an office door at all. The
   door of my office has been taken off. [*He goes to the door of his office,
   wrenches it off and flings it offstage*] After twelve o'clock I'm ready to see
   any one of you . . . any one who's got a problem, general or personal,
   can come to me and I'll solve it for him, any problem of any kind, be it
   even some matrimonial problem. He can come to me after twelve

o'clock. It should be understood by you that we are here in order to work. [*Shouting*] To work!

The EMPLOYEES *immerse themselves in the papers placed before them and work quickly and earnestly.* DR WAHID *sits at his desk.* UNCLE HUSSEIN, BASSIOUNI *and* MITWALLI *enter; they are amazed and at a loss for words.*

HUSSEIN: Dr Wahid.

DR WAHID: At your service, Uncle Hussein.

HUSSEIN: I want to work on the project.

DR WAHID: At your service. What would you like to work at?

HUSSEIN: [*Angrily*] Work at? This is my project.

DR WAHID: Come now, Uncle Hussein. You mustn't say that. This project belongs to all of us, it belongs to the whole country.

BASSIOUNI: Isn't that so, Dr Wahid? By the Prophet, tell him.

DR WAHID: Actually, I've already told him and he didn't like it.

HUSSEIN: [*Confused*] I'm sorry. That's not exactly what I meant. My point is . . . I must work here.

DR WAHID: I'm prepared to support you in anything you ask. You know, if only you had a doctorate in Egyptology like me, you'd long ago have been in charge of the project.

HUSSEIN: My dear sir, I don't want to be in charge of anything.

DR WAHID: Listen here, Uncle Hussein . . . I've got it. Just so you won't say I'm not on your side, I'll employ you in accordance with your experience.

HUSSEIN: Meaning what?

DR WAHID: I'll let you take over the project's canteen. It's true the regulations say that we must put it out to tender and invite bids for running the canteen, but I'll break the rules for your sake and bear the responsibility. Happy, my dear sir?

HUSSEIN: [*Lowering his head slightly*] I'm prepared to work on anything to do with the project just so that the wheat can be distributed.

DR WAHID: It will be distributed. Be sure of that. After all, what am I sitting here for?

BASSIOUNI: My problem's a simple one, Dr Wahid. I'm a student affiliated to the Faculty of Commerce and could therefore work on the accounts.

DR WAHID: [*Taking out a card on which is written the number '8'*]
Here you are, my dear sir. I've appointed you in Accounts. From now on your name is Number Eight.

BASSIOUNI *hangs the number round his neck and sits down happily at his desk.*

DR WAHID: [*Pointing at* MITWALLI] And you, my boy?

MITWALLI: No, I don't want anything. I'm with Uncle Hussein.

BASSIOUNI: [*Noticing* UNCLE HUSSEIN *and* MITWALLI *going out*] Hussein! Hussein! Please be so good as to bring me a coffee . . . medium-sugared.

UNCLE HUSSEIN *looks at him for a long time and does not reply.* MITWALLI *answers sorrowfully.*

MITWALLI: Certainly, Mr Bassiouni. Certainly.

BASSIOUNI: Don't say Mr Bassiouni . . . I'm now Number Eight.

MITWALLI: Certainly, Number Eight.

They both go out. The clock strikes twelve, and no sooner have the strokes sounded than BASSIOUNI *rushes up to the Director's desk, with an application in his hand.*

BASSIOUNI: [*With excessive politeness*] Sir, I have a problem that keeps me awake at night . . . it affects my output and could well throw the project's accounts into confusion.

DR WAHID: What is it?

BASSIOUNI: I'm a student affiliated to the Faculty of Commerce and I've got to attend the lectures because otherwise I won't pass. I therefore ask that Your Honour transfer me to the head office in Cairo so that I can be near to the Faculty, in the interests of my future.

DR WAHID: [*In a loud voice as he initials his application*] That's it, my dear sir. Number Eight is to be transferred to the head office in Cairo near to his Faculty, in the interests of his future.

BASSIOUNI *takes the application with great joy and while going out meets* MITWALLI *who has come with his coffee. Standing, he sips at it hastily.*

BASSIOUNI: [*Very exhilarated*] Do you know, Mitwalli, I've been transferred to Cairo. Now I'm Number Eight. When I take my B.A. I'll become Number Five. If I make a real effort and take an M.A. I'd become Number Three, and if I were to sit down and get stuck into a doctorate I'd be promoted and replace Dr Wahid. You stay here and let Uncle Hussein help you.

He rushes out while MITWALLI *watches with a look of intense surprise, then he too goes out with a shrug of his shoulders. The* EMPLOYEES *stand about singly so that each one of them may tell his problem, then they gather round the Director in a circle that grows gradually narrower and narrower as, carrying their applications, they wave them in the Director's face as though they were swords. All the* EMPLOYEES *are talking at once, trying to explain their problems. The circle around the Director grows narrower, while their voices grow gradually louder.*

EMPLOYEE ONE: The latest Republican Decree says that failure to achieve a higher grade shall operate for six years only and that one then takes the grade together with the increment, but Staff Administration is insistent on giving me either the increment or the grade, whichever is less. In such an event my colleague, who was appointed at the same time as myself in the Ministry of Agriculture, will have his salary increased by thirty piastres, and thus Your Honour should demand that we have equal treatment with our colleagues in other ministries, or you should at least give me a long holiday during which I can go to Cairo and put right my position.

EMPLOYEE TWO: My wife was appointed to the Ministry of Education three years ago. I was appointed to Cairo and she was appointed to Zagazig. I made an application asking that either I be appointed with her in Zagazig or that she be appointed to Cairo. It appeared though that there were no archaeological sites in Zagazig for me to go to, and that the schools in Cairo were sufficiently staffed already. Afterwards I was suddenly transferred here in the desert. Of course my wife cannot be transferred here in the desert because there are no schools, while I can't go to Zagazig because there are no archaeological sites there. I would therefore request Your Honour either to make some schools here for my wife or to make some archaeological sites in Zagazig, or, alternatively, to transfer both of us to Cairo.

EMPLOYEE THREE: Sir, I am a graduate of the Cinema Institute, the Photographic Section, and I stayed for two years without working. You see, sir, there are some old types who are in control of all film work and they don't want any new blood to enter the cinema field. Afterwards I applied to the Labour Office, the one near me here, but I don't yet know what I'll be working at here. I would thus request Your Honour to let me set up a photographic section. Your Honour knows how full the desert here is of extremely beautiful and fascinating views. What I mean is that we could make a photographic section with modern equipment which would cost at the most five thousand pounds, and then we could photograph the views and sell them to the tourists and we'd get back the costs of the section within ten years, and after that we'd produce films that wouldn't cost a thing.

EMPLOYEE FOUR: I was going to have a loan of twenty thousand pounds . . . that's two years ago and then I was transferred here suddenly before I handed over the documents, and afterwards, as I was coming in the train, the wind blew away all the documents into the desert. If I don't hand over these documents I'll be in serious trouble. I would therefore ask Your Honour to inform the frontier guards to look round for the documents, or to inform the Air Force, or to defray the costs of a camel and one guide and to give me a month's leave in which I myself may search for the documents, or for Your Honour to transfer me to Cairo so I can get other documents prepared.

EMPLOYEE FIVE: I, sir, have come to point out to Your Honour that we here are entitled to desert allowances or allowances in respect of the nature of the work along the lines of our colleagues in the New Valley. I would also point out to Your Honour that there are sums remaining over from the old budget; we must take advantage of these sums or else they'll go back to the Treasury. My opinion is that we should use them to build rest-houses and that we should bring refrigerators, bottled gas and heaters here.

EMPLOYEE SIX: I, sir, don't have any problems, but it doesn't make sense that one should let a chance like this go by without talking or at least joining with one's colleagues in a situation like this. And so I add my voice to those of my colleagues who have problems so that Your Honour can solve these problems. However if you don't intend to solve these problems, then I'll send a complaint to Cairo right away and let them knock the living daylights out of you, 'cos it doesn't make sense to chuck us out into the desert and send us someone in charge who doesn't solve our problems.

Their voices grow louder. When they reach shouting pitch they divide into two opposing teams, as they give the traditional call: Za . . . ma . . . lek, etc.

DR WAHID: That's enough. Shut up, all of you, you fools . . . it's unreasonable, I can't believe it . . . I can't imagine it . . . I can't conceive of it . . . it's not reasonable that there are people like you still living in the country . . . You people they've sent to co-operate with me in a project like this . . . are you people human beings? What's all this rubbish about Zamalek and Al-Ahli? [*He challenges them emphatically*] Ismailia must go to the top of the league this year.* What do you think you're saying . . . What are you talking about? I swear by God, seeing as how things have reached this pitch, I swear I'll divorce my wife if I stay here a minute longer. I'll send you Doctor Wahid-Hyphen who'll make you forget all about football . . . who'll show you what's what.

Having finished talking, he springs off the top of his desk and leaves the stage. The EMPLOYEES *leave in embarrassment and return to their desks. After a moment* DR WAHID-HYPHEN *enters, dressed in white and adorned with a long blue sash. He begins to examine the place and the employees, then claps his hands in despair.*

DR WAHID-HYPHEN: [*Reassuring himself*] Never mind, never mind. Everything will be put to rights. Never mind. Listen here . . . I'd like to present myself to you: I'm Dr Wahid-Hyphen, and despite my great respect for Dr Wahid [*with scorn*] who's got no hyphen, though he used to be my professor, I am nevertheless unable to believe that it's he who made such a mess of arranging the desks. He is certainly a specialist in the arranging of desks, but the way he's arranged this set-up of yours is quite wrong. Yes, it's wrong and if it was he who arranged them in this way, then he's an ass of a man. It doesn't make sense that Number Five should sit next to Number Six . . . I mean, suppose Number Seven wants to draw the attention of Number Five, how does he do it? Anyway, it'll all come out all right in the end . . . It'll come out all right . . . What's been done badly can be put to rights . . . I don't want anyone to lose heart . . . there's still a chance to put matters right . . . Be careful not to lose heart, my boys . . . Come along and help me. Number Five to sit in Number Three's place . . . and Four in Number Five's . . . and Six in Eight's . . . quick about it, we haven't much time . . . Three in Two's place . . . Two in Five's . . . come along, quickly.

---

*Ismailia is the name of another football team.

The EMPLOYEES *quickly change places and there's a great deal of bustle on stage. When, however, they eventually settle down we notice that they are sitting exactly in the same places as they were before.*

DR WAHID-HYPHEN: Thanks be to God. Finally I've put right the error. Do you know, my friends, the work wouldn't have been of any use with the arrangement as at first. Now everyone is sitting in his right place . . . and don't think that I'm the person who deserves the credit for having brought this about. No, the idea came to me from you . . . I derived my inspiration from you. If you hadn't helped me by being so quick and not losing heart, it would not have been possible for us to have had such a success. May God bless us. God will put everything right. Put your trust in God.

UNCLE HUSSEIN *and* MITWALLI *enter. They are carrying two trays of coffees. Directly* DR WAHID-HYPHEN *sees them he gets into a violent temper and becomes like a raging bull.*

DR WAHID-HYPHEN: What's this? What's all this? It's wrong . . . wrong . . . wrong. It's a crime. What you're doing is a crime. [*He directs his words to the employees*] Listen, sirs. Now listen here, you two . . . there's to be no such thing as a canteen. The government gives you your salary for the six hours you work: six hours by sixty minutes by sixty seconds. Understood? When you drink tea and coffee and waste ten minutes or a quarter of an hour of the state's time, you become a thief . . . This canteen's to be closed immediately . . . it's to be closed with sealing wax. [*Directing his words at* UNCLE HUSSEIN *and* MITWALLI] Listen, you over there, I don't want to see you again. Understood? You and your lad are to get out of here at once . . . at once.
HUSSEIN: Can I say a word?
DR WAHID-HYPHEN: Not a word.
HUSSEIN: Give me a chance . . .
DR WAHID-HYPHEN: Not so much as a syllable . . . Be sure not to open your mouth. What would you say after all? Sssss . . . shut up . . . Not a word . . . If you've paid down a guarantee for the canteen, I'll give it back to you . . . just put in a claim. If the employees have ordered things on credit with you, then come along and get paid for them on the first of the month. Hush! That's enough . . . shut your mouth . . . not a word.
HUSSEIN: Let's come to an understanding.

DR WAHID-HYPHEN: What are we going to come to an understanding about? Have I got the time to talk nonsense? Hush . . . not a word.

HUSSEIN: [*Pulling* MITWALLI *by the arm*] Let's get going, Mitwalli. Throw them their napkins.

They go out.

DR WAHID-HYPHEN: What a crazy idea to have a canteen! [*He sits at his desk*] Now let's have a look at the post . . . [*He reads for a while*] Listen, good sirs, here's a letter from Cairo asking what production's up to.

EMPLOYEES: Production of what?

DR WAHID-HYPHEN: Production of what? Don't you know of what?

ALL EMPLOYEES: No. Doesn't Your Honour know?

DR WAHID-HYPHEN: How should I know if Dr Wahid had you all seated wrong and didn't leave a memorandum saying what the project was about?

ALL EMPLOYEES: Your Honour doesn't know?

DR WAHID-HYPHEN: It's I who am asking. All right, if you don't know, what are you coming here to work at?

ALL EMPLOYEES: That we really do know.

DR WAHID-HYPHEN: Thanks be to God. Let's go at it step by step, seeing as how you know what you're working at. In this way, we'll know what this project is, and so we'll know what production's up to. Listen, my boy, what are you working at?

EMPLOYEE ONE: Emoluments.

DR WAHID-HYPHEN: And you?

EMPLOYEE TWO: Increments.

DR WAHID-HYPHEN: And you?

EMPLOYEE THREE: Documents.

DR WAHID-HYPHEN: And you?

EMPLOYEE FOUR: Assignments.

DR WAHID-HYPHEN: And you?

EMPLOYEE FIVE: Allotments.

DR WAHID-HYPHEN: And you?

EMPLOYEE SIX: Disbursements.

DR WAHID-HYPHEN'*s questions follow one another and the* EMPLOYEES *answer them solely with the syllable 'ments'.*

DR WAHID-HYPHEN: [*In a state of great agitation*] It's all a plot against me. You want to get me into serious trouble. All of you are 'ments' . . . 'ments' . . . 'ments' . . . and none of you knows what the project is! At any rate I refuse to despair. I must work it out for myself. [*He thinks*] We're now in the desert. So the project's one of two things: land reclamation or oil. But, heavens, we're Egyptologists . . . and this area hasn't got any archaeological sites at all. Antiquities aren't measured by bushels . . . and yet the letter asks . . . [*He looks at the letter*] . . . How is production in terms of bushels? This can drive you crazy . . . [*He turns to them shouting*] All right, listen here: which of you arrived here first? Think.

ALL EMPLOYEES: We all came together.

DR WAHID-HYPHEN: It doesn't make sense . . . it's impossible . . . think . . . I beseech you . . . don't land me in trouble.

EMPLOYEE ONE: Ah, I've thought . . . when I came I sat at this desk . . . [*remembering with difficulty*]

DR WAHID-HYPHEN: Yes?

EMPLOYEE ONE: When I first came to sit at this desk, the fellow who's called Mitwalli brought me a coffee with medium sugar. Which means that the canteen people had opened up the canteen before we got here . . . meaning that this project was first of all a canteen.

DR WAHID-HYPHEN: [*Shouting*] Go after them. What are you waiting for? Go after them in a jeep and bring them to me at once.

Some of the EMPLOYEES *go out and immediately return with* UNCLE HUSSEIN *and* MITWALLI, *holding on to them as though they were criminals.*

DR WAHID-HYPHEN: Let them be . . . come along . . . you wait, Uncle Hussein. Come here and sit down Mitwalli, my boy. [MITWALLI *sits down*] Mitwalli, were you here before those employees came?

MITWALLI: Yes.

DR WAHID-HYPHEN: Who was with you?

MITWALLI: Uncle Hussein.

DR WAHID-HYPHEN: What were you doing?

MITWALLI: We were boring in the desert.

DR WAHID-HYPHEN: What were you looking for?

MITWALLI: Uncle Hussein says there's wheat . . .

DR WAHID-HYPHEN: [*Interrupting him as he suddenly remembers*] Ah, the wheateries. [*To the employees*] How can you make me forget like that?

Of course, having been seated wrongly, it took all my energy to rearrange you. How could I forget something like that? The newspapers went on talking about the subject for nearly a month. Thanks a lot, Mitwalli. Have a seat, Uncle Hussein. Please . . . honestly . . . you must take my place.

UNCLE HUSSEIN *sits in* DR WAHID-HYPHEN's *chair, while the Doctor sits on the edge of the desk.*

DR WAHID-HYPHEN: What sort of coffee will you have, Uncle Hussein? Or would you like something cold?

HUSSEIN: Where from? The canteen's been closed down.

DR WAHID-HYPHEN: No, don't worry, I've made my arrangements . . . [*He produces three small thermos flasks from the drawer of his desk*] Coffee, tea or something cold?

HUSSEIN: No, thank you.

DR WAHID-HYPHEN: Uncle Hussein, where's the wheat?

HUSSEIN: What wheat?

DR WAHID-HYPHEN: The wheat that's under the ground?

HUSSEIN: [*Greatly astonished*] Wheat under the ground? Who said anything about that?

DR WAHID-HYPHEN: You of course.

HUSSEIN: In what capacity would I say that? I was someone who used to be in charge of a canteen.

DR WAHID-HYPHEN: And the wheateries?

HUSSEIN: What wheateries, Doctor? Have you gone off your head? Is wheat to be found under the ground.

DR WAHID-HYPHEN: Where is it found, then?

HUSSEIN: They grow it of course. According to my information about wheat it's grown. This is something that Your Honour would of course have studied in primary school. Everyone must know that wheat is grown. If you came here wanting wheat, then go ahead and grow it. Come on, Mitwalli, let's get going.

The EMPLOYEES *are immersed in their work.* DR WAHID-HYPHEN *stands up, struck dumb with astonishment.* UNCLE HUSSEIN *and* MITALLI *are in the circle of light at the front of the stage.*

MITWALLI: Why didn't you tell him, Uncle Hussein?

HUSSEIN: He's a good-for-nothing that man. If he'd been half human he'd have given me the chance to speak before turning us out. A man who doesn't give the person in front of him the right to speak, whatever the circumstances, is not someone to be trusted. Perhaps, if I did tell him, I'd find the wheat had become a cake wrapped around in cellophane and sold in Zamalek.*

MITWALLI: And then?

HUSSEIN: And then what? I shall stay on in the desert. I shall look around for a cave and sit there and have a think. I shall look for a way in which to get the wheat to the people without going through that lot. I must find a way.

MITWALLI: And I'll stay with you, Uncle Hussein.

HUSSEIN: No, Mitwalli. Bassiouni has assured his future, and I would like to assure your future. Listen, Mitwalli, your feet, are they still golden? Don't you still know how to take a good shot at goal?

MITWALLI: I can go up the wing, dribble through the backs, and shoot a goal.

HUSSEIN: Right, I'll give you a card to a friend of mine who looks after the cafeteria at a very large club. You go and tell him 'I've been sent by Uncle Hussein'. I want you to have a very good breakfast before you go, and in a matter of a couple of months you'll do more than Bassiouni will be able to do in twelve years. Goodbye, Mitwalli.

As the curtain goes down we hear a commentator's voice saying: 'The man's who's going out on the field now is that artist . . . that maestro . . . that technician . . . the cunning fox . . . that first-class goal scorer . . . Mitwalli . . . Mitwalli . . . the man with the golden foot.' The shouting of the crowds grows louder: 'Look . . . see . . . Mitwalli's scored again!'

CURTAIN

---

*Zamalek is the upper-class district of Cairo from which the football team takes its name.

The Donkey Market

Tewfik al-Hakim

The Donkey Market *by Tewfik al-Hakim*

Cast

TWO UNEMPLOYED MEN

FARMER

FARMER'S WIFE

Scene 1: *Near the donkey market. From afar is heard the braying of donkeys. Outside the market sit two men whose ragged clothes and filthy appearance indicate that they are out-of-work loafers.*

FIRST UNEMPLOYED: [*To his companion*] Are you able to tell me what the difference is between us and donkeys?

SECOND UNEMPLOYED: You can hear the difference with your own ears.

FIRST UNEMPLOYED: The braying?

SECOND UNEMPLOYED: Just so, the braying.

FIRST UNEMPLOYED: Couldn't this braying be donkey talk?

SECOND UNEMPLOYED: That's what it must be.

FIRST UNEMPLOYED: So they're talking now.

SECOND UNEMPLOYED: Maybe they're also shouting.

FIRST UNEMPLOYED: I wonder what they're saying?

SECOND UNEMPLOYED: You'd have to be a donkey to know that.

FIRST UNEMPLOYED: They talk to each other so loudly.

SECOND UNEMPLOYED: Naturally, don't they have to hear each other?

FIRST UNEMPLOYED: I thought donkeys whispered together.

SECOND UNEMPLOYED: Why? Why should they?

FIRST UNEMPLOYED: Just like us.

SECOND UNEMPLOYED: Don't worry . . . donkeys aren't like us.

FIRST UNEMPLOYED: You're quite right, donkeys are a civilised species.

SECOND UNEMPLOYED: What are you saying? Civilised?

FIRST UNEMPLOYED: Have you ever seen wild donkeys? There are wild horses and wild buffaloes and wild pigeons and wild cats, but ever since donkeys have been going around amongst us they've been working peacefully and talking freely.

SECOND UNEMPLOYED: Freely?

FIRST UNEMPLOYED: I mean aloud.

SECOND UNEMPLOYED: Talking about aloud, can you tell me why we aren't able to live decently, your goodself and my goodself?

FIRST UNEMPLOYED: Because your goodself and my goodself are broke.

SECOND UNEMPLOYED: And why are we broke?

FIRST UNEMPLOYED: Because no one gives a damn about us. If only we had a market like this donkey market, someone would buy us.

SECOND UNEMPLOYED: And why doesn't anybody buy us?

FIRST UNEMPLOYED: Because we're local merchandise.

SECOND UNEMPLOYED: What's wrong with that?

FIRST UNEMPLOYED: There's only money for foreign merchandise.

SECOND UNEMPLOYED: Why don't we go off and advertise ourselves?

FIRST UNEMPLOYED: How?

SECOND UNEMPLOYED: With our voices.

FIRST UNEMPLOYED: They wouldn't come out loud enough.

SECOND UNEMPLOYED: How is it that a donkey's voice comes out all right?

FIRST UNEMPLOYED: Because, as I told you, they're a civilised species.

SECOND UNEMPLOYED: You've got me interested. Oh, if only I were a donkey, like this one coming along! Look over there . . . the donkey being led along by the man who's taking it out from the market. I wonder how much he paid for it! Look how proud and cock-a-hoop he is as he takes it away!

FIRST UNEMPLOYED: I've had an idea.

SECOND UNEMPLOYED: What is it?

FIRST UNEMPLOYED: Would you like to become a donkey?

SECOND UNEMPLOYED: Me? How?

FIRST UNEMPLOYED: Don't ask questions. Would you like to or wouldn't you?

SECOND UNEMPLOYED: I'd like to, but how?

FIRST UNEMPLOYED: I'll tell you. You see the donkey that's coming towards us, being led by the man who bought it. Well, I'll go up to the man and distract him by chatting him up. At the same time you undo the rope round the donkey's neck without its owner noticing and tie it round your own neck.

SECOND UNEMPLOYED: That's all? And then what?

FIRST UNEMPLOYED: And then he'll lead you off and I'll lead off the donkey.

SECOND UNEMPLOYED: And where will he lead me off to?

FIRST UNEMPLOYED: I wouldn't be knowing, that's in the lap of the gods.

SECOND UNEMPLOYED: Are you talking seriously?

FIRST UNEMPLOYED: Isn't it you who want it this way?

SECOND UNEMPLOYED: I tie a rope round my neck and he leads me away?

FIRST UNEMPLOYED: And what's wrong with that? At least you'll have found yourself someone to guarantee that you get a bite to eat.

SECOND UNEMPLOYED: It won't be what you call a bite . . . more like a munch.

FIRST UNEMPLOYED: It's all the same . . . just something to eat.

SECOND UNEMPLOYED: As you say, it'll be a change from being hungry and without a roof over one's head. But how am I going to put myself over to the man?

FIRST UNEMPLOYED: That depends on how smart you are.

SECOND UNEMPLOYED: We'll have a go.

FIRST UNEMPLOYED: Hide yourself . . . the man mustn't catch sight of us together.

The two men part and the stage is empty. A man – he looks like a farmer – appears. He holds a rope with which he is leading a donkey. The FIRST UNEMPLOYED *approaches him.*

FIRST UNEMPLOYED: Peace be upon you!

FARMER: And upon you be peace!

FIRST UNEMPLOYED: Good God, man, is it that you don't know me or what?

FARMER: You . . . who would you be?

FIRST UNEMPLOYED: Who would I be? Didn't we break bread together?

FARMER: I don't understand. You mean to say we once broke bread together?

FIRST UNEMPLOYED: You mean you've forgotten all that quickly? No one but a bastard forgets a good turn.

FARMER: Are you calling me a bastard?

FIRST UNEMPLOYED: May God strike dead anyone who said such a thing about you. What I meant was that anyone who forgets his friends . . . but then, thank God, you're a really decent and civil person, it's merely that it's just slipped your mind what I look like. The point is that we met at night, over dinner, and it just happened the moon wasn't out that night.

FARMER: The moon? When? Where?

FIRST UNEMPLOYED: I'll remind you. Just be patient till the knot's untied.

He looks furtively at his companion who has slipped by unnoticed and is engrossed in undoing the knot of the rope.

FARMER: What's untied?

FIRST UNEMPLOYED: I'm tongue-tied. You've embarrassed me, you've made me forget what I was saying. Give me some help. [*Stealing a glance at his companion and urging him to hurry up*] Get the knot untied and do me the favour of getting me out of this.

FARMER: I can't understand a thing you're saying.

FIRST UNEMPLOYED: You'll understand soon enough . . . once the knot's untied, which it must be . . . things have gone on for a long time . . . far too long. Man, get it untied quickly.

FARMER: But what shall I untie?

FIRST UNEMPLOYED: [*Seeing that his companion has finished undoing the rope and has tied it round his neck and let the donkey loose*] Well, it's finally got untied all right. It's the Almighty God Himself who unties and solves things. Everything is untied and solved in its own good time. Everything has its time, and seeing as how you don't remember me now I'll leave you time in which to think it over at your leisure. God willing, we'll be meeting up soon and you'll remember me and you'll give me a real warm welcome. Peace be upon you.

He leaves the FARMER *in a state of confusion. He goes behind the donkey, takes it and moves off without being noticed.*

FARMER: [*To himself*] Where did I meet him? Where did we have dinner? The moon wasn't out? Could be . . . these days one's mind wanders a bit.

He pulls at the donkey's halter so as to lead it away, not knowing that the SECOND UNEMPLOYED *has taken the donkey's place.*

FARMER: [*Calling out*] C'mon, donkey.

The SECOND UNEMPLOYED *imitates the braying of a donkey.*

FARMER: [*Looking round and being startled*] Hey, what's this? Who are you?

SECOND UNEMPLOYED: I'm the donkey.

FARMER: Donkey?

SECOND UNEMPLOYED: Yes, the donkey you've just bought at the market.

FARMER: It's impossible!

SECOND UNEMPLOYED: Why are you so surprised? Didn't you just buy me at the market?

FARMER: Yes, but . . .

SECOND UNEMPLOYED: But what?

FARMER: In the name of God the Merciful, the Compassionate!

SECOND UNEMPLOYED: Don't be frightened, I'm your donkey all right.

FARMER: How? . . . you're human.

SECOND UNEMPLOYED: It's your destiny, your good luck.

FARMER: Are you really human or are you . . . ?

SECOND UNEMPLOYED: Yes, human, not a genie. Don't worry, it can all be explained. Just calm down a bit.

FARMER: I . . . I've calmed down.

SECOND UNEMPLOYED: Listen, then, my dear sir . . . the explanation is that my father . . . a nice fellow like your goodself . . . was, however, real stubborn and got it into his head to marry me off to a girl I'd never seen and who'd never seen me. I refused but he still insisted. I suggested to him that we talk it over and come to some sort of understanding, that it had to be discussed in a spirit of freedom. He got angry and said, 'I won't have sons of mine arguing with me.' I said to him, 'I refuse to accept what you're saying.' So he said to me, 'You're an ass.' I said to him 'I'm not an ass.' He said, 'I said you're an ass and you've got to be an ass,' and he called upon God to turn me into an ass. It seems that at that moment the doors of Heaven were open and the prayer was answered and I was actually turned into a donkey. My father died and they found me in the livestock fold, having become part of his estate. They sold me at the market and you came along and bought me.

FARMER: Extraordinary! Then you are the donkey I bought?

SECOND UNEMPLOYED: The very same.

FARMER: And how is it that you're now back again as a human being?

SECOND UNEMPLOYED: I told you, it's your destiny, your good luck. It seems you're one of those godly people and the good Lord, may He be praised and exalted, decided to honour you . . .

FARMER: Really! But what's to be done now?

SECOND UNEMPLOYED: What's happened?

FARMER: What's happened is that you . . . is that I . . . I don't know how to go about things. What I mean to say is that I've lost my money, I'm ruined.

SECOND UNEMPLOYED: You haven't lost a thing.

FARMER: How's that?

SECOND UNEMPLOYED: Didn't you buy yourself a donkey? The donkey's right here.

FARMER: Where is he?

SECOND UNEMPLOYED: And where have I gone to?

FARMER: You?

SECOND UNEMPLOYED: Yes, me.

FARMER: You want to tell me that you're . . .

SECOND UNEMPLOYED: Wholly your property. You bought me with your money on the understanding I'm a donkey. The deal was concluded. Let's suppose that after that I turn into something else, that's no fault of yours. You've made a purchase and that's the end of it.

FARMER: Yes, I bought . . .

SECOND UNEMPLOYED: That's it . . . relax.

FARMER: You mean to say you're my property now?

SECOND UNEMPLOYED: In accordance with the law. I'm yours by right. Right's right . . . and yours is guaranteed.

FARMER: Fair enough. Good, so let's get going.

SECOND UNEMPLOYED: At your disposal.

FARMER: Turn here, O . . . Hey, what shall I call you?

SECOND UNEMPLOYED: Call me by any name. For instance, there's . . . there's Hassawi.[1] What d'you think of that for a name? Hassawi . . . come, Hassawi . . . go Hassawi!

FARMER: Hassawi?

SECOND UNEMPLOYED: It's relevant!

FARMER: May it have God's blessings. Let's go then . . . Mr Hassawi! Wait a moment, I think this business of the rope round your neck isn't really necessary.

SECOND UNEMPLOYED: As you think best.

FARMER: Better do without the rope . . . after all where would you go to? Wait while I undo it from round your neck.

SECOND UNEMPLOYED: [Undoing the rope himself] Allow me. Allow me . . . if you'd be so good.

FARMER: Yes, that's right. Come along, let's go home, Mr . . . Hassawi.

---

[1] Hassawi is a well-known breed of riding donkey in Egypt.

Scene 2 *Inside the farmer's house his* WIFE *is occupied with various household jobs. She hears knocking at the door.*

WIFE: Who is it?

FARMER: [*From outside*] Me, woman. Open up.

WIFE: [*Opens the door and her husband enters*] You were all this time at the market?

FARMER: I've only just got back.

WIFE: You bought the donkey?

FARMER: I bought . . .

WIFE: You put it into the fold?

FARMER: What fold are you talking about, woman? Come along in, Mr Hassawi.

WIFE: You've got a guest with you?

FARMER: Not a guest. He's what you might . . . I'll tell you later.

WIFE: Please come in.

FARMER: Off you go and make me a glass of tea.

The WIFE *goes off.*

HASSAWI: [*Looking around him*] It seems I . . .

FARMER: And what shall I say to my wife?

HASSAWI: Tell her the truth.

FARMER: The truth?

HASSAWI: Exactly . . . not a word more and not a word less. There's nothing better than plain-speaking.

FARMER: And where will you be sleeping in that case?

HASSAWI: In the fold.

FARMER: What do you mean 'the fold'? Do you think that's right?

HASSAWI: That's where I belong. Don't change the order of things. The only thing is that if you've a mattress and a pillow you could put them down for me there.

FARMER: Fine, but what about food? It's not reasonable for you to eat straw, clover and beans.

HASSAWI: I'll eat beans . . . just as long as they're broad beans.

FARMER: With a little oil over them?

HASSAWI: And a slice of lemon.

FARMER: And you'll go on eating beans forever?

HASSAWI: It's all a blessing from God!

FARMER: Just as you say. Donkeys have just the one food. They don't know the difference between breakfast, lunch and dinner. It's straw and clover and beans and that's all.

HASSAWI: I know that.

FARMER: Fine, we've settled your sleeping and your food. Tell me now, what work are you going to do?

HASSAWI: All work donkeys do . . . except being ridden.

FARMER: Ridden?

HASSAWI: You can't ride me because you'd only fall off.

FARMER: And carrying things? For example I was intending taking a load of radishes and leeks on the donkey to the vegetable merchant.

HASSAWI: I'll do that job.

FARMER: You'll carry the vegetables on your shoulders?

HASSAWI: That's my business. I'll manage. I may be a donkey but I've got a brain.

FARMER: Brain? I was forgetting this question of a brain.

HASSAWI: Don't worry, this brain of mine's at your service. You can always rely on me. Just give me confidence and the right to talk things over with you freely.

FARMER: Meaning you can go on your own to the merchant with the produce?

HASSAWI: And agree for you the best price with him.

FARMER: We'll see.

WIFE: [*From outside*] Tea!

HASSAWI: If you'll excuse me.

FARMER: Where are you going?

HASSAWI: I'm going to inspect the fold I'm sleeping in.

FARMER: You'll find it on your right as you go out.

HASSAWI *goes out. The* WIFE *enters with the glass of tea.*

WIFE: [*Giving the tea to her husband*] Your guest has gone out?

FARMER: He's not a guest, woman. He's . . .

WIFE: What?

FARMER: He'd be a . . . a . . .

WIFE: Be a what?

FARMER: He's a . . . a . . .

WIFE: Who is he?

FARMER: You won't believe it.

WIFE: What won't I believe?

FARMER: What I'll tell you now.

WIFE: All right then, just tell me.

FARMER: He's . . . the donkey I bought.

WIFE: The donkey?

FARMER: Yes, didn't I go to the donkey market today to buy a donkey? He's the donkey I bought at the market.

WIFE: Man, do you want to make an utter fool of me?

FARMER: Didn't I tell you that you wouldn't believe me?

WIFE: But what shall I believe . . . that the market's selling human donkeys?

FARMER: He wasn't a human at the time I bought him . . . he was a donkey like the rest . . . and he was braying.

WIFE: He brays as well?

FARMER: Yes, by God, I swear by the Holy Book he was braying.

WIFE: And then?

FARMER: And then on the way home . . . I was leading him by the rope . . . I turned round and found that he'd changed into a human.

WIFE: God save us! . . . an afreet!

FARMER: No, woman, he's no *afreet* . . . he was transformed. Originally he was a human being, the son of decent folk like ourselves. He was then transformed into a donkey and they sold him off at the market. I bought him and God, may He be praised and exalted, decided to honour me so He turned him back into a human.

WIFE: Your omnipotence, O Lord!

FARMER: Well, that's what happened.

WIFE: But after all . . .

FARMER: What? What do you want to say?

WIFE: Nothing.

FARMER: No, there's something you want to say.

WIFE: I want to say . . . what I mean is . . . is . . . what are we going to do with him now, with him being a . . . a human being?

FARMER: Do what with him? Exactly as with any other donkey . . . and in addition to that he's got a brain as well.

WIFE: I suppose we won't be able to ride him?

FARMER: Let's forget about the question of riding for the moment.

WIFE: And we'll talk to him as with other human beings?

FARMER: Yes, talk to him and call him by his name.

WIFE: He's got a name?

FARMER: Of course, what do you think? His name's Hassawi. We'll call him and say to him, 'Come here, Hassawi; go there, Hassawi.'

WIFE: And where will he sleep?

FARMER: In the fold. You can put a mattress out for him there.

WIFE: And what will he eat?

FARMER: Beans . . . but with oil.

WIFE: With oil?

FARMER: And lemon.

WIFE: And he drinks tea?

FARMER: Let's not get him used to that.

WIFE: How lovely! . . . we've got a human donkey!

FARMER: Be careful, woman not to say such things to the neighbours or they'll be saying we've gone off our heads!

WIFE: And what shall I say to them?

FARMER: Say . . . say for example that he's a relative of ours from far away who's come to help us with the work during these few days just as we're coming into the month of Ramadan.

A knock at the door.

WIFE: Who is it?

HASSAWI: [*From outside*] Me . . . Hassawi.

WIFE: [*To her husband*] It's him!

FARMER: Open the door for him.

WIFE: [*Opens the door*] Come in . . . and wipe your feet on the doorstep.

HASSAWI: [*Entering*] I've cleaned myself a corner in the fold and spread it out with straw.

FARMER: There you are, my dear lady, he cleans up and makes his own bed . . . yet another advantage.

WIFE: Yes, let him get used to doing that.

HASSAWI: I was coming about an important matter.

FARMER: To do with what?

HASSAWI: To do with the vegetable merchant.

FARMER: The vegetable merchant? What about him?

HASSAWI: A man came on his behalf . . . I just met him at the door and he said the merchant was in a hurry to take delivery. I got him talking and understood that the prices of radishes and leeks would go up in Ramadan. I told him that you were still giving the matter your

consideration because there's a new buyer who's offered you a better
price. The man was shaken and immediately said that he was prepared
to raise the price he was offering.

FARMER: He said so?

HASSAWI: [*Producing some money*] I took a higher price from him. Here
you are!

FARMER: God bless you!

HASSAWI: But I have a request to make of you.

FARMER: What is it?

HASSAWI: Would you allow me, before you decide definitely about
something, to talk the matter over with you freely and frankly?

FARMER: I'm listening.

HASSAWI: Were you intending to hand over the whole crop to the
merchant?

FARMER: Yes, the whole of it.

HASSAWI: Why?

FARMER: Because we need the money.

HASSAWI: Is it absolutely necessary at the present time?

FARMER: Yes it is. We're in dire need of money as we come up to
Ramadan. Have you forgotten the dried fruits, the mixed nuts and the
dried apricot paste we need to buy?

HASSAWI: I've had an idea.

FARMER: Let's have it.

HASSAWI: We set apart a portion of the crop and have it for seed for the
new sowing instead of buying seed at a high price during the sowing
season.

FARMER: It's a long long time until the new sowing.

WIFE: The Lord will look after the new sowing . . . we're living in today.

HASSAWI: As you say. In any event I've given you my opinion . . . I'm just
afraid the time for the new sowing will come and you won't have the
money to pay for the seeds and you'll have to borrow at interest or go off
to a money-lender, and perhaps you'll be forced to sell me in the market.

FARMER: Let God look after such things.

WIFE: What's he talk so much for?

FARMER: [*To* HASSAWI] Have you got anything else to say?

HASSAWI: Yes, I'm frightened . . .

FARMER: What are you frightened about? Tell us and let happen what may!

HASSAWI: Yes, I must say what I have in my mind and clear my conscience.
As I was passing by your field just now I noticed that the feddans sown

under radishes and leeks had at least ten kerats lying fallow because the irrigation water isn't reaching there.

FARMER: And what can we do about that?

HASSAWI: It needs one or two shadoofs.

FARMER: We thought about it.

HASSAWI: And what stopped you?

FARMER: Money . . . where's the money?

HASSAWI: [*Looking at the* WIFE's *wrist*] Just one of the lady's bracelets . . .

WIFE: [*Shouting*] Ruination!

HASSAWI: By putting ten kerats under irrigation you'll get the price of the bracelet back from the first sowing.

FARMER: You think so?

WIFE: [*Beating her chest*] What disaster! Man, are you thinking of listening to what that animal has to say? Are you seriously thinking of selling my bracelets?

FARMER: We haven't yet bought or sold anything . . . we're just talking things over.

WIFE: Talking things over with your donkey, you sheep of a man?

FARMER: What's wrong with that? Let me hear what he has to say . . . you too.

WIFE: Me listen? Listen to that? Listen to that nonsensical talk that gives you an ache in the belly? He's been nothing but an ache in the belly from the moment he came.

FARMER: He's entitled to his opinion.

WIFE: His opinion? What opinion would that be? That thing has an opinion? Are we to be dictated to by the opinion of a donkey in the fold?

FARMER: He's not like other donkeys.

WIFE: So what! I swear by Him who created and fashioned you that if that donkey of yours doesn't take himself off and keep his hands away from my bracelets I'll not stay on under this roof!

FARMER: Be sensible and calm down. After all, have we agreed to go along with his opinion?

WIFE: That was all that was missing . . . for you to go along with his opinion! All your life you've been master in your own house and your word has been law. Then off you go to the market and come back dragging along behind you your dear friend Mr Hassawi, whose every opinion you listen to.

FARMER: His opinions and help have gained for us an increase in price from the merchant.

WIFE: An increase? He won't allow us to enjoy it. He wants to waste it all on his crazy ideas, just as we're about to have all the expenses of Ramadan . . . and then don't forget there's the Feast directly after Ramadan and for which we'll need cake . . .

FARMER: And after the cake for the Feast we'll have to face up to the Big Feast for which we'll need a sheep.

WIFE: Knowing this as you do, why do you listen to his talk?

FARMER: Listening doesn't do any harm.

WIFE: Who said so? A lot of buzzing in the ears is worse than magic.

FARMER: What you're saying is that we should tell him to keep his mouth shut?

WIFE: With lock and bolt . . . and put a sock in it! He's a donkey and must remain a donkey and you're the master of the house and must remain master of the house. You're not some tassel on a saddlebag at this time of life. Have some pride, man . . . you, with your grey hairs!

FARMER: So I'm a tassel on a saddlebag?

WIFE: You're getting that way, I swear it. Your dear friend Hassawi is almost all-powerful here.

FARMER: How all-powerful, woman? I still have the reins in my hand.

HASSAWI: [*To himself*] The reins?

WIFE: All right, what are you waiting for? Why don't you put the bridle on him as from now?

FARMER: And what does it matter if we let him ramble on as he wants?

HASSAWI: [*To himself*] Ramble on?

WIFE: I'm frightened of all this rambling and rumbling of his.

FARMER: What are you frightened of?

WIFE: That he'll try to fool you and you'll believe him.

FARMER: Believe him? Why should I? Who said I was a donkey?

WIFE: The donkey's there in front of you and he's had his say.

FARMER: Talking's one thing and action's another.

WIFE: What action are you talking about . . . you've let the rope go.

FARMER: You're saying I should tie him by the neck?

WIFE: Like every other donkey.

FARMER: But he's human, woman.

WIFE: Originally he was a donkey. When you bought him from the donkey market, when you paid good money for him, he was a donkey, and so his place is out there in the fold and he mustn't enter the house or have a say in things. That's how it should be. If you don't like it I'll go out and call upon the neighbours to bear witness. I'll say to them: 'Come to my rescue, folk . . . my man's gone crazy in the head and has bought a donkey from the market which he's made into a human and whose opinions he's listening to.'

FARMER: Don't be mad, woman!

WIFE: By the Prophet, I'll do it . . .

FARMER: All right, keep quiet . . . that's it!

WIFE: What d'you mean, 'That's it'? Explain!

FARMER: We'll go back to how we were and relax. Hey, you, Hassawi, listen here!

HASSAWI: Sir!

FARMER: See, this business of my asking your opinion and your asking mine doesn't work. I'm the man with the say-so round here, and all you've got to do is obey. What I mean is that that mouth of yours mustn't utter a word . . . understand? Go off to the fold while I arrange about your work.

HASSAWI: Certainly, but would you just allow me to say something . . . one last word?

WIFE: What cheek! He's told you that you shouldn't talk, that you should keep your mouth closed and shut up. You really are a cheeky fellow!

HASSAWI: That's it, then . . . I've closed my mouth and shut up. With your permission. [*He goes out*]

Scene 3 *Outside the door of the* FARMER*'s house* HASSAWI *suddenly sees his companion, the* FIRST UNEMPLOYED, *approaching and leading the original donkey. The two friends embrace.*

HASSAWI: [*To his companion*] Tell me . . . what did you do?

FIRST UNEMPLOYED: And you? How did you get on?

HASSAWI: I'll tell you right now. How, though, did you know I was here?

FIRST UNEMPLOYED: I walked along far behind you without your noticing. Tell me . . . what happened with our friend the owner of the donkey?

HASSAWI: You're well rid of him. He's an idiotic man who doesn't know where his own good lies. And why have you now come back with the donkey?

FIRST UNEMPLOYED: We don't need it. Things are settled . . . the good Lord's settled them.

HASSAWI: How's that?

FIRST UNEMPLOYED: We've found work.

HASSAWI: You've found work?

FIRST UNEMPLOYED: For you and me.

HASSAWI: Where? Tell me quickly!

FIRST UNEMPLOYED: After I left you and went off, I and the donkey, I found a large field where there were people sowing. I said them: 'Have you got any work.' 'Lots,' they said . . . 'for you and ten like you.' I said to them: 'I've got someone with me.' 'You're welcome,' they said to me, 'Go and bring him along immediately and start working.' So I came to you right away.

HASSAWI: Extraordinary! There we were absolutely dying to get work, remember? People used to look at us and say 'Off with you, you down-and-out tramps, off with the two of you . . we've got no work for down-and-outs!'

FIRST UNEMPLOYED: It seems that having the donkey alongside me improved my reputation!

HASSAWI: You're right. Don't people always say 'He works like a donkey'? A donkey means work just as a horse means honour. Don't people say that the riding of horses brings honour, that dogs are good guards, and that cats are thieves?

FIRST UNEMPLOYED: Yes, by God, that's right. They saw me with the donkey and said to themselves, 'He can't be a down-and-out tramp . . . he must be one for hard work,' so they took me on my face value and you sight unseen . . . on the basis of my recommendation!

HASSAWI: Your recommendation or the donkey's?

FIRST UNEMPLOYED: The donkey's. It actually got the work for both you and me. Isn't it only fair that we should return it to its owner?

HASSAWI: That's only fair.

FIRST UNEMPLOYED: What shall we say to him?

HASSAWI: We'll tell him to take back his donkey.

FIRST UNEMPLOYED: And you . . . didn't you pretend to be his donkey and tie the halter round your neck?

HASSAWI: He'll now prefer the real donkey.

FIRST UNEMPLOYED: Look, instead of handing over the donkey to him and getting into all sorts of arguments, with him asking us where the donkey was and where we were, we'll tie the donkey up for him in front of his house and clear off. What d'you think?

HASSAWI: Much the best idea . . . let's get going.

They tie the donkey to the door of the house, then knock at the door and disappear from view. The door opens and the FARMER *appears.*

FARMER: [*Sees the donkey and is astonished and shouts*] Come along, woman!

WIFE: [*Appearing at the door*] What's up?

FARMER: Look and see!

WIFE: What?

FARMER: He's been transformed again . . . Hassawi's become a donkey like he was at the market. He's exactly the same as he was when I bought him.

WIFE: Thanks be to God . . . how generous you are, O Lord!

FARMER: Yes, but . . .

WIFE: But what? What else do you want to say?

FARMER: But we're the cause.

WIFE: Why, though? What did we do to him?

FARMER: We did the same as his father did to him . . . he silenced him and turned him into a donkey!

WIFE: And what's wrong with him being a donkey? At least we can ride him.

FARMER: You're right. When he was a human with a brain he was useless for riding.

WIFE: And what did we need his brain for? What we want is something to ride, something that's going to bear our weight and take us from one place to another. Give thanks to the Lord, man, for returning your useful donkey to you.

FARMER: [*Gently stroking the donkey's head*] Don't hold it against us, Hassawi! Fate's like that. I hope you're not annoyed. For us, though, you're still as you were . . . Mr Hassawi.

WIFE: Are you still at it, man? Are you still murmuring sweet nothings to that donkey? Mind . . . he'll go back to speaking again!

The FARMER *leads his donkey away in silence towards the fold, while the* WIFE *lets out shrill cries of joy.*

CURTAIN